WHY

AMERICA

HATES BIBLICAL CHRISTIANITY

HATES BIBLICAL CHRISTIANITY

Pursuing Christlikeness
in Times of Mounting Hostility and Apathy

DAVID A. HARRELL

Authentic Christianity has never been held in high esteem by the unbelieving world—and we're told not to be surprised by this (1 John 3:13). It is certainly not a new problem or a historical anomaly. Jesus said, "The world . . . hated Me before it hated you" (John 15:18). He went on to explain why that hatred is so profound and persistent: "Because they do not know the One who sent Me" (v. 21).

So the unbelieving world's contempt for biblical truth is not a dispute that can be settled through a culture war. It is not a public-relations problem to be solved by adjusting our message. It is not a political difficulty that we can vote away. It is not an intellectual obstacle we can help the unbeliever think around. It is a clash between two spiritual kingdoms that are fundamentally opposed to one another at every level.

The intensifying ferocity of the world's disdain for Christ is a reminder of our duty to "wage the good warfare" (1 Timothy 1:18). But this is not a conflict against flesh and blood; it is a rescue mission for the hearts and souls of people who are imprisoned by false ideologies and twisted worldviews (2 Corinthians 10:4-5). Dave Harrell understands this, and he skillfully shows from Scripture how true followers of Christ should respond—and why we must remain steadfast—even as the moral fabric of American society is unraveling all around us.

JOHN MACARTHUR
Pastor-Teacher, Grace Community Church; Chancellor, The Master's University and Seminary

I deeply appreciate Dave Harrell's clear, insightful, encouraging analysis of our culture's spiritual meltdown, and our duty as Christians to respond with courage and conviction. If you are troubled or confused by the erosion of American culture and the rise of militant unbelief, I'm certain you will be emboldened and uplifted by this excellent book.

PHIL JOHNSON
Executive Director, Grace to You

Why America Hates Biblical Christianity by David A. Harrell is a timely and important book for all Christians who are concerned about the direction of this great nation. In eight chapters, Harrell deals with the Christian's allegiance, affection, authority, assembly, adversary, assurance, ambition, and aspiration. Modern events, including the 2020 presidential election results, are analyzed and addressed from a scriptural perspective. This book is well written, well researched, and engaging. It is easy to read while covering matters that are heart-wrenching for Christians who long for the United States of America to return to her Christian roots. This is a book which will be instructive and inspirational for all God-fearing Christians.

DR. DEWEY ROBERTS
Pastor of Cornerstone Presbyterian Church in Destin, FL;
Moderator of Vanguard Presbytery; Executive Director of Church Planting International; Author of *Samuel Davies: Apostle to Virginia* and *Historic Christianity and The Federal Vision*

Why America Hates Biblical Christianity
Pursuing Christlikeness in Times of Mounting
Hostility and Apathy

ISBNS:
978-1-63342-237-7 paper
978-1-63342-238-4 epub
978-1-63342-239-1 mobi

Cover design and typeset by www.greatwriting.org

Printed in the United States of America

Shepherd Press
P.O. Box 24
Wapwallopen, PA 18660
www.shepherdpress.com

This book is published jointly with Shepherd's Fire. Shepherd's
Fire exists to proclaim the unsearchable riches of Christ through
mass communications for the teaching ministry of Bible expos-
itor David Harrell, with special emphasis in encouraging and
strengthening pastors and church leaders.
www.shepherdsfire.org

Contents

Introduction 10

The Christian's Allegiance 16

The Christian's Affection 36

The Christian's Authority 62

The Christian's Assembly 88

The Christian's Adversary 110

The Christian's Assurance 136

The Christian's Ambition 162

The Christian's Aspiration 190

Appendix 216

To my Father

Edgar A. Harrell

The most godly and giving man I have ever known

Acknowledgments

....

I wish to express my sincere appreciation to Jim Holmes, Acquisitions Editor at Shepherd Press, for his keen theological insights and wise input in the editorial process of this manuscript. His love for Christ, his unwavering devotion to the truth of Scripture, his godly character, and his burden for the lost continue to be a source of great encouragement to me and an invaluable resource to the true church of Jesus Christ. His friendship and willingness to co-laborer with me is a very tangible expression of God's grace in my life, one for which I am eternally grateful.

I also wish to thank Tedd and Aaron Tripp at Shepherd Press for their willingness to publish this work for the salvation of sinners, the edification and encouragement of the saints, and the glory of Christ.

Introduction

Why America Hates Biblical Christianity

*But realize this, that in the last days difficult times will come.
For men will be lovers of self, lovers of money, boastful,
arrogant, revilers, disobedient to parents, ungrateful, unholy,
unloving, irreconcilable, malicious gossips, without self-control,
brutal, haters of good, treacherous, reckless, conceited, lovers
of pleasure rather than lovers of God, holding to a form of
godliness, although they have denied its power. . .*

2 Timothy 3:1-5a

"*Dave, what has happened to our country? This is not the country I fought for. Surely the Lord will not tolerate this much longer.*" I have heard these three short sentences literally hundreds of times over the last twenty years. They are the heartfelt words of my ninety-six-year-old father (born in 1924)—the sorrowful lament of a decorated WWII Marine who fought in the Pacific theater aboard the USS *INDIANAPOLIS* and survived her sinking (the greatest naval catastrophe at sea in the history of the Navy),[1] a recipient of the Congressional Gold Medal and, more importantly, a godly man with a deep love for Christ and a longing for His return.

Like millions of other Americans, the nightly scenes of ANTIFA and Black Lives Matter "protestors" looting, burning, tearing down statues, and attacking police officers appall him. He's dumbfounded by the draconian Coronavirus lockdown orders that are destroying far more lives than the virus itself. He's horrified by the 62 million babies that have been aborted since 1973 when the U.S. Supreme Court ruled that the Constitution of the United States protects a pregnant woman's liberty to have her inconvenient and unwanted baby brutally dismembered.[2] He shakes his head in disgust as he watches our country plunge into an abyss of immorality and gender confusion. And like so many he asks, "Why are so many evangelicals supporting these things?"

Who would have thought that a nation founded upon Judeo-Christian ethics would stray so far that by 2020 only 6 percent of Americans would possess a biblical worldview?[3] Yet here we are.

As a pastor, I grieve over all this. Hopefully you do, too. And I especially grieve for those who reject the one true and living God of the Bible—those who walk in spiritual darkness, enslaved by their sinful lusts and who have the wrath of an infinitely holy God abiding on them. I have a passion to see them reconciled to

---

1 I have written a book about this entitled, *Out of the Depths: An Unforgettable WWII Story of Survival, Courage, and the Sinking of the USS INDIANAPOLIS* (Bethany House Publishers; a division of Baker Publishing Group, Minneapolis, Minnesota, 2014).

2 https://www.nationalrighttolifenews.org/2020/08/abortion-statistics-united-states-data-and-trends-4/

3 https://www.christianpost.com/news/record-low-number-of-americans-hold-biblical-worldview-survey-says.html

God through faith in Christ and enjoy the blessings that come to all who love Him.

Moreover, frustrated by the ignorance, worldliness, fear, and apathy that characterize so many Christians, I yearn for the true church to be discerning, encouraged, hopeful, and evangelistic. I have an intense longing for Christ's kingdom to come and His will to be done on earth as it is in heaven—the only solution to all the problems that afflict the world, problems that can be seen most vividly in the culture war that is dividing and destroying our country.

Ordinary people can easily see that there has been a concerted effort by the liberal establishment in America to eliminate religious influence in society—especially the godly morality and gospel message of biblical Christianity. I use the term "biblical" to describe true, genuine, authentic Christianity, in contrast to the many counterfeit forms of Christianity that have plagued the world since the birth of the church at Pentecost. For indeed, Jesus warned "Not everyone who says to Me, 'Lord, Lord,' will enter the kingdom of heaven, but he who does the will of My Father who is in heaven will enter" (Matt. 7:21).

For the most part, America is now a post-Christian nation. Its culture now embraces the beliefs of postmodernism where people no longer believe in *absolute* or *moral truth* and instead become skeptical in their beliefs, subjective in their values, and consider truth to be something relative. As a result, all viewpoints—no matter how absurd and contradictory—must be considered equally valid, unless, of course, they derive their authority from the Bible. Like never before in American history, Christians are witnessing biblical values being replaced by laws that impose a godless, immoral, oppressive social agenda on their country—laws that now even suppress religious freedoms guaranteed in the First Amendment of the Bill of Rights.

The practical implications of these rulings combined with the overall disdain political and religious liberal activists have for conservative values have ignited an epic culture war that is now raging out of control. Civility in public discourse is gone. Rage has replaced reason. Facts mean nothing. Evil is called good and good is called evil. Anarchists are destroying cities. Police are being attacked and killed, along with many innocent people. Millions of citizens are bewildered, angry, and afraid. It is little wonder that gun and ammunition manufacturers cannot keep up with the demand as citizens arm themselves.

To be sure, America is now in an ideological civil war that threatens the very survival of the nation. But many people sense there's something more sinister going on, something beyond the realm of ideological divides, something evil, perhaps even eschatological. Conspiracy theories abound. Distrust of government and media is unprecedented. People—including many evangelical Christians—are looking for answers. As a pastor, I deal with these matters on a daily basis, and this why I decided to write this book. It's not that I have any answers in myself—nor does anyone else—but because I know the Word of God. God alone has the answers, and He alone will reveal them to those "who [are] humble and contrite of spirit, and who tremble at [His] word" (Isa. 66:2).

God has revealed to us what many fail to realize and most will never admit: there are two corresponding evils that have been secretly gaining strength in America for many years; powers that have destroyed every empire in history; powers so formidable and so deceptive that they now threaten the Constitutional Republic of the United States. With an irrepressible malignity, these deadly agents are destroying every institution that has made this country exceptional. From our public schools, colleges, and universities, to our system of government, these silent enemies continue to metastasize, even to the point of destroying the nuclear family, the foundation stone of society. And what are the names of these twin evils? *Human depravity* and *Satanic deception*. One is an enemy *in* us; the other is an enemy *of* us. And they both find a place to reside in *secular government* and in *false religion*. They are twin fiends that are always united against the gospel of God and the people of God.

The purpose of this book is therefore twofold. First, to demonstrate the interplay between *human depravity* and *Satanic deception* from a biblical perspective and show how they manifest themselves in our culture—especially in the ideologies of the political left and the liberalism of many who claim to be Christians. This will explain *Why America Hates Biblical Christianity*.

Second, to encourage authentic Christians to become more like Christ by examining eight doctrinal themes that help define biblical Christianity. Only then can we love our enemies. Only then will our hearts be filled with excitement and expectation, even in days of mounting hostility, as we await the return of our glorious King in fulfillment of His promise:

> There will be no end to the increase of His government or of peace, on the throne of David and over his kingdom, to establish it and to uphold it with justice and righteousness from then on and forevermore.
> (Isa. 9:7)

1

. . . .

The Christian's Allegiance

Two Opposing Kings and Kingdoms

Now to the King eternal, immortal, invisible, the only God,
be honor and glory forever and ever. Amen.
1 Timothy 1:17

Let Us Burn Our Babies

···

The sound of drums has a powerful effect. Whether in a military parade, a marching band, a climactic tympani roll at the end of a symphony, or a ceremonial war dance, the loud rhythmic beating of percussion instruments has a way of drowning out everything else in the realm of our sensory perception. Such was the intention of "the high places of Topheth, which is in the valley of the son of Hinnom" (Jer. 7:31), an east-west valley at the south end of Jerusalem. The term "Tophet" comes from the Hebrew word *toph* for "drum." This is significant because it was in the Valley of Hinnom where the ancient people of Judah sacrificed their children to the idol of Molech by throwing them alive into a burning fire while drums were beaten to drown out their screams. With holy outrage God described this horror saying,

> They have built the high places of Topheth, which is in the valley of the son of Hinnom, to burn their sons and their daughters in the fire, which I did not command, and it did not come into My mind.
> (Jer. 7:31)

In Jesus' day, the Valley of Hinnom was also called Gehenna, a garbage dump where fires burned continually—a place of massacre and perpetual flames that became an apt symbol of the eternal fires of hell, which Jesus described as *"pyros geenan"* translated "fiery hell" (Matt. 5:22).

It is incomprehensible that anyone could commit such a ghastly crime against an innocent child. But such is the power of satanic deception. They actually believed that such an act of barbarism would cause the Canaanite god Molech to reward them (2 Kings 23:10). Although they knew it was an abomination to God (Jer. 32:34-35), clearly forbidden in His law (Lev. 18:21) and punishable by death (Lev. 20:2), they foolishly believed it was in their best interest and therefore rejected God's pathway to blessing. While unimaginably awful, this is where Judah's religious apostasy had led them. They had no fear of God. They scoffed at His law and thought they were above it. So with a seared conscience they were comfortable with this depraved practice—one that is no different than when millions of preborn infants are brutally sacrificed every year to the god of self on the altar of personal expediency and corporate profits.

Judah's idolatry ultimately resulted in divine judgment, a fate that will befall all the peoples of the world who mock the one true God. His pronouncement of judgment upon them was truly terrifying:

> "Because they have forsaken Me and have made this an alien place and have burned sacrifices in it to other gods, that neither they nor their forefathers nor the kings of Judah had ever known, and because they have filled this place with the blood of the innocent and have built the high places of Baal to burn their sons in the fire as burnt offerings to Baal, a thing which I never commanded or spoke of, nor did it ever enter My mind; therefore, behold, days are coming," declares the LORD, "when this place will no longer be called Topheth or the valley of Ben-hinnom, but rather the valley of Slaughter. I will make void the counsel of Judah and Jerusalem in this place, and I will cause them to fall by the sword before their enemies and by the hand of those who seek their life; and I will give over their carcasses as food for the birds of the sky and the beasts of the earth. I will also make this city a desolation and an object of hissing; everyone who passes by it will be astonished and hiss because of all its disasters. I will make them eat the flesh of their sons and the flesh of their daughters, and they will eat one another's flesh in the siege and in the distress with which their enemies and those who seek their life will distress them."
> (Jer. 19:4–9)

Would God Owe a Nation an Apology?

As prophesied in 586 BC, God's wrath was eventually poured out upon them at the hands of the Babylonians (Jer. 39, 40, 52), but not without great sorrow on His part. He longed for them to repent and promised to forgive them—a theme illustrated throughout Jeremiah's prophecy causing him to be called "the weeping prophet" (9:1; 14:17). In light of His judgment on His covenant people, *if God doesn't judge America, He will owe Judah an apology.* But sadly, unregenerate people can't fathom any of this. The god they worship (if they worship one at all) bears no resemblance to the infinitely holy God who has revealed Himself in creation, in Scripture, and in the person of the Lord Jesus Christ. Theirs is an idol—a god of their own making made in their image, a god of love—according to their definition—who winks at sin and would never punish anyone.

For people who refuse to worship Christ, the torturous slaughter of an innocent infant is a small sacrifice to offer to gain personal pleasure and prosperity, especially for those who have no spiritual and moral authority any higher than their own ideas. A great example of this is the testimony of the well-known American singer-songwriter Stevie Nicks who said "abortion rights" were her generation's "fight." She described the great benefit of an abortion she had in 1979, saying, "If I had not had that abortion, I'm pretty sure there would have been no Fleetwood Mac. There's just no way that I could have had a child then, working as hard as we worked constantly. . . and there were a lot of drugs, I was doing a lot of drugs . . . I would have had to walk away." The abortion was "really important" to her because "the music we were going to bring to the world was going to heal so many people's hearts and make people so happy" and there "was not another band in the world that has two lead women singers, two lead women writers."[4]

Christians are appalled with such a statement. And our hearts ache with pity for so many like Stevie Nicks who mock God's law, live only for themselves, and scoff at the idea of divine judgment. Yet this is the prevailing mindset of America. Most people will applaud her and viciously attack anyone who dissents. Who can forget the massive marches in Washington where women wore pink hats shaped like female genitalia as a symbol of support and solidarity for women's rights and political resistance—especially the right to abortion on demand?

---

4 https://www.christianpost.com/news/stevie-nicks-without-my-abortion-no-fleetwood-mac.html

Why the Differences in Our Culture?

So why the vast difference in moral values? Why the immense cavern between, for example, liberal Democrats who will fight to the death to preserve a woman's "right to choose" (along with many other forms of moral degeneracy) and the values of conservative Christians who find these things unconscionable? Why are Judeo-Christian principles—the very foundation of our country—under siege? Why are Bible-believing Christians increasingly marginalized and maligned in our culture? Why is there such a growing appetite for government to control all we think and do?

While the answer is multifaceted, at its very core is the influence of the invisible forces of the *kingdom of Satan* at war with the *kingdom of God*. Thankfully, God will ultimately prevail to the praise of his glory. Indeed, a day is coming when "at the name of Jesus every knee will bow, of those who are in heaven and on earth and under the earth, and . . . every tongue will confess that Jesus Christ is Lord, to the glory of God the Father (Phil. 2:10–11).

Most evangelicals have little understanding of these opposing kingdoms and are apathetic toward them. Non-Christians consider them laughably absurd—which is to be expected since they have no capacity to discern the things of the Spirit of God (1 Cor. 2:14). Moreover, Satan "the god of this world has blinded the minds of the unbelieving so that they might not see the light of the gospel of the glory of Christ, who is the image of God" (2 Cor. 4:4). Nevertheless, neither ignorance nor apathy nor even rejection of the truth changes the fact that it is true. Understanding the power, purpose, and future of these opposing kingdoms will expose the greatest of all conspiracy theories. But unlike most others, this one is not only *true,* but it also determines the eternal destiny of people's souls.

The Kingdom of God

While there is much more agreement than disagreement among Christians concerning God's kingdom program, there is an ongoing debate concerning certain aspects of it, especially as it relates to the thousand-year reign of Christ in Revelation 20 (and that will be discussed later). This is due to differing assumptions in interpretation that influence how we understand language and the Bible—a science and art of interpretation called *hermeneutics.*

While the particulars of this debate are beyond the purview and purpose of this book (but are briefly addressed in Appendix A), I believe it is important for you to understand my position, which will be duly noted and obviously shape how I view certain aspects of God's kingdom program. But beyond these distinctions—which should never be viewed as a test of orthodoxy—every genuine Christian affirms God's sovereign reign over all He has created and His ultimate triumph over Satan's temporary kingdom reign. Together, we all sing with full-throated praise:

> *Crown him with many crowns,*
> *The Lamb upon his throne.*
> *Hark! How the heavenly anthem drowns*
> *All music but its own.*
> *Awake, my soul, and sing of him*
> *Who died for thee,*
> *And hail him as thy matchless King*
> *Through all eternity.*

Three Aspects of the Kingdom of God

The *Kingdom of God* is, in my view, the primary theme of Scripture—the center of gravity around which all other themes providentially orbit in bringing glory to the "King of kings, and Lord of lords" (Rev. 19:16). This is what makes it so important and exciting! There are essentially three aspects to the Kingdom of God: *a Universal Kingdom,* a *Mediatorial Kingdom,* and a *Spiritual Kingdom.* A general understanding of God's kingdom program will help explain much of the moral free fall in America and the mounting hostility toward all who oppose it. But more importantly, it will animate the hearts of the redeemed with a renewed passion to see our Savior and King face-to-face.

1. The Universal Kingdom of God

First, God's *Universal Kingdom* can be defined as *God's eternal sovereign rule over all that exists*. In David's great song of majesty and love he said, "Your kingdom is an everlasting kingdom, and Your dominion endures throughout all generations" (Ps. 145:13). It is universal in scope where God rules in absolute sovereignty over all His creation. "The LORD has established His throne in the heavens, and His sovereignty rules over all" (Ps. 103:19; *cf.* 10:16; 22:28; 59:13). Such transcendence renders earthly governments and arrogant rulers puny by comparison. In his magnificent prayer of praise, David acknowledged God's universal reign saying,

> Yours, O LORD, is the greatness and the power and the glory and the victory and the majesty, indeed everything that is in the heavens and the earth; Yours is the dominion, O LORD, and You exalt Yourself as head over all. Both riches and honor come from You, and You rule over all, and in Your hand is power and might; and it lies in Your hand to make great and to strengthen everyone.
> (1 Chron. 29:11–12)

Knowing that God is ultimately reigning over all that exists brings great comfort to Christians who have placed their faith in the One who will ultimately triumph over all that is wrong in the world and gather His redeemed to Himself in the indescribable splendor of heaven. We see this expressed in David's doxology recorded in 1 Chronicles 29:10–13:

> So David blessed the LORD in the sight of all the assembly; and David said, "Blessed are You, O LORD God of Israel our father, forever and ever. Yours, O LORD, is the greatness and the power and the glory and the victory and the majesty, indeed everything that is in the heavens and the earth; Yours is the dominion, O LORD, and You exalt Yourself as head over all. Both riches and honor come from You, and You rule over all, and in Your hand is power and might; and it lies in Your

hand to make great and to strengthen everyone. Now therefore, our God, we thank You, and praise Your glorious name."

I trust these truths will also cause you to bless the LORD. Can there be any greater joy than knowing that our Redeemer lives and reigns and is coming again? I think not. In his own inimitable style, Charles Spurgeon has remarked,

This living Jesus is . . . raised to an eminence of glory and power. He does not now sorrow as "a humble man before his foes," nor labour as "the carpenter's son"; but He is exalted far above principalities and power and every name that is named. The Father has given Him all power in Heaven and in earth, and he exercises this high endowment in carrying out His work of grace. . . the glory which surrounds the ascended Lord should breathe hope into every believer's breast. Jesus is no mean person—He is "a Saviour and a great one." He is the crowned and enthroned Redeemer of men. The sovereign prerogative of life and death is vested in Him; the Father has put all men under the mediatorial government of the Son, so that He can quicken whom He will. He openeth, and no man shutteth. At His word the soul which is bound by the cords of sin and condemnation can be unloosed in a moment. He stretches out the silver scepter, and whosoever touches it lives.[5]

2. The Mediatorial Kingdom of God

Second, Scripture also affirms another aspect of God's universal kingdom, a *Mediatorial Kingdom* that can be defined as *God's sovereign rule over the earth through divinely chosen human representatives who speak on His behalf and who represent the people before Him.*[6] Here God exercises absolute authority in His invisible, spiritual kingdom on earth through the agency of divinely chosen men. He gave them special revelation that they recorded in Scripture to explain His kingdom purposes and how sinners can enter it.

5 Charles Spurgeon, *All of Grace* (Chapter 14, "My Redeemer Liveth"), https://www.monergism.com/thethreshold/sdg/spurgeon/allgrace.pdf
6 Alva J. McClain, *The Greatness of the Kingdom*, (Winona Lake, Indiana; BMH, 1959), 41.

By continuing the narrative of the Old Testament prophets, the New Testament helps us understand that the final *Mediatorial Kingdom* will include a literal, thousand-year reign of Christ upon the earth (Rev. 20:4–6) where He will rule as the Last Adam. This final reign of Christ upon the earth—often called the *Millennial Reign of Christ* or the *Messianic Kingdom*—will finally transform everything on this planet into conformity with the perfect will of God and His *Universal Kingdom* and therefore be the consummating bridge between human history and the eternal kingdom described in Revelation 21:1–22:5.

Anticipating the ultimate rule of the One who is so routinely mocked and ignored is a profound encouragement to every Christian who loves Christ and longs for His return. In the words of the prophet Habakkuk, we eagerly await the day when "the earth will be filled with the knowledge of the glory of the LORD, as the waters cover the sea" (2:14).

What the World Needs Now

To be sure, unbelievers are clueless about these things, and many believers really don't care. No wonder so many people are hopeless, depressed, and eaten up by a gnawing sense of emptiness. They're looking for answers, but don't know where to turn. I was reminded of this by the lyrics of an old song that came to mind—*What the world needs now is love sweet love, It's the only thing that there's just too little of.* While I appreciate the sentiment, what the world needs now is a love all right, but not some sentimental love as it is typically defined. *What the world needs now is a love for God* "who so loved the world, He gave His only begotten Son, that whoever believes in Him shall not perish but have eternal life" (John 3:16). The world needs a self-denying, saving love for the only Savior and coming King, Jesus Christ, who even now rules in absolute sovereignty over His universal kingdom. Though it currently suffers the effect of His curse on sin and groans under the weight of those who resist Him, He will prevail in the end. And He gives this warning to those who oppose Him:

Remember this, and be assured;
Recall it to mind, you transgressors.
Remember the former things long past,
For I am God, and there is no other;
I am God, and there is no one like Me,
Declaring the end from the beginning,
And from ancient times things which have not been done,
Saying, "My purpose will be established, and I will accomplish all My good pleasure."
(Isa. 46:8–10)

The Big Issue: Who Is Jesus Christ?

Atheists, agnostics, and deists who believe in God but reject Christ will constantly make sanctimonious references to God. Many politicians will even refer to themselves as a "person of faith." But they will avoid like the plague any reference to the Lord Jesus Christ. If pressed, Americans as a whole vehemently reject the following truths about Jesus Christ:

- He is the Son of God (Phil. 2:5–8; Col. 2:9)
- He is the creator and sustainer of all things (John 1:3; Col. 1:15–17; Heb. 1:2)
- He is the redeemer of all who place their faith in His sacrificial death on the cross (John 10:15; Rom. 3:24–25; 5:8; 1 Peter 2:24)
- He is the only mediator between God and man (1 Tim. 2:5)
- He is the only way to salvation (Acts 4:12; John 14:6)
- He is the head of His body the church (Eph. 1:22; 5:23; Col. 1:18)
- He is the coming universal King who will reign on the throne of David forever (Isa. 9:6; Luke 1:31–33)
- He is the final judge of all who reject Him as Lord and Savior (Matt. 25:14–46; Acts 17:30–31)

Therefore, all other religions that deny these truths are false and all who embrace them will be condemned to eternal wrath (John 3:36). This is one of the primary reasons America hates

25

biblical Christianity. The gospel message is horribly offensive to self-righteous sinners, "to Jews a stumbling block and to Gentiles foolishness, but to those who are the called, both Jews and Greeks, Christ the power of God and the wisdom of God" (1 Cor. 1:23–24). I pray that every reader will come to Christ in faith for forgiveness, peace, and eternal life. God "justifies the ungodly" (Rom. 4:5), and "pardons iniquity . . . because He delights in unchanging love" (Mic. 7:18).

3. The Spiritual Kingdom of God

In addition to the *universal* and *mediatorial* aspects of God's kingdom program, Scripture also reveals a *spiritual kingdom* that can be defined *as an invisible kingdom that exists only in the hearts of those who have trusted in Jesus Christ, the King.* However, this aspect of the kingdom came after Israel rejected their Messiah. Furthermore, while the kingdom of God can have spiritual requirements and characteristics (see Rom. 14:17), this does not rule out the land and physical prosperity promises that are also included in the Abrahamic, Davidic, and New covenants (Jer. 31–33; Ezek. 36–37; *cf.* Deut. 30:1–10). Some historical background will be helpful in understanding these astounding promises.

At the beginning of the New Testament era, the Jewish people were like Simeon who was "looking for the consolation of Israel" (Luke 2:25). The angel Gabriel told Mary she would give birth to a Son who would be great and sit on the throne of his father David and rule over Israel forever (Luke 1:32–33). Zacharias, the father of John the Baptist (the forerunner to the Messiah who prepared the way for his coming [Luke 1:16–17]), prophesied that with his coming, God was fulfilling "His holy covenant, the oath which He swore to our father Abraham" (Luke 1:72–73) which would include the deliverance of Israel from her enemies (v. 74). So Messianic kingdom expectations dominated the thinking of first-century Israel. Naturally, they longed for their King to free them from the bondage of Rome and establish His glorious kingdom on earth. But they didn't understand that repentance was required for them to gain entrance into His kingdom (Matt. 5–7). Furthermore, they could not fathom that their Messiah must first be a sin-bearing servant before He could be "exalted and extolled and be very high" (Isa. 52:13) and rule over His kingdom (see Isa. 52:13-15; 53:1-12).

At first, both King Jesus and His herald, John the Baptist, preached the same kingdom message of the Old Testament prophets saying, "Repent, for the kingdom of heaven is at hand" (Matt. 3:2; 4:17). Jesus even performed miraculous signs and wonders to authenticate His regal credentials. But they rejected both their King and His message (Matt. 11:20-24) resulting in catastrophic judgment at the hands of the Romans in AD 70 (Matt. 23:37-39; Luke 19:41-44). After Israel's rejection, the promised earthly kingdom was postponed, and Jesus began to reveal new truths about the spiritual aspect of His kingdom program. He began speaking in parables (Matt. 13) and spoke of the "mysteries of the kingdom of heaven" (Matt. 13:11), and of a future kingdom that would be established upon His return (Luke 19:11-27) after a period of great tribulation on earth (Luke 21:31).

The Pharisees were looking for visible signs to validate Jesus' claims to be the Messiah (Luke 17). But Jesus wanted them to understand that the *spiritual kingdom* is internal and not marked by observable signs (vv. 20b-21) like those that will be seen when He establishes His reign on earth. For this reason Jesus told Nicodemus, the leading teacher of Israel, "Truly, truly, I say to you, unless one is born again he cannot see the kingdom of God" (John 3:3; *cf.* Matt. 13:11-16). This was primarily a reference to the prophesied messianic kingdom at the end of the age that the Pharisees and the Jewish people eagerly awaited (Isa. 11:1-6; Dan. 12:2), also described as the "regeneration" of the world (Matt. 19:28).

But what the Jews failed to understand is that apart from spiritual regeneration, no one can enter the *messianic kingdom* at Christ's second coming—that time when His glory and that of the redeemed (Rom. 8:19-21; 1 John 3:2) will be made visible to all (Rev. 1:7; *cf.* 19:11-21). In His first coming, Jesus came as the Suffering Servant, and His death on the cross established the basis for the *regeneration of sinners* and His rule within their hearts. But the *regeneration of all things* will not occur until His second coming when He will be revealed in all his glory—not as a *Suffering Servant*, but as the *Sovereign King*.

During the forty days between Jesus' resurrection and ascension, He "[spoke] of the things concerning the kingdom of God" (Acts 1:3), a reference to His spiritual kingdom—the sphere of salvation where God reigns in the hearts of believers who experience the new covenant spiritual blessings of a new heart and of the indwelling Spirit who "gives life" (2 Cor. 3:6). The New Testament epistles reveal how entrance into the *spiritual kingdom* comes through the message of the gospel and is granted to all believers in this church age. This *was* and *is* the great evangelistic message of the church that America rejects.

For example, Philip came "preaching the good news about the kingdom of God" (Acts 8:12). Paul also "entered the synagogue and continued speaking out boldly for three months, reasoning and persuading them about the kingdom of God" (Acts 19:8; *cf.* 28:23). He also warned the Corinthians that "the unrighteous will not inherit the kingdom of God" (1 Cor. 6:9; *cf.* Gal. 5:21; Eph. 5:5). Indeed, true kingdom citizens will be marked by "righteousness and peace and joy in the Holy Spirit" (Rom. 14:17)—a stark contrast to those who dwell in the *Kingdom of Satan*.

The Kingdom of Satan

A cosmic battle has been raging between Satan and God from the beginning of time and will continue to the end of time. He has opposed the kingdom purposes of God since the first sin in the cosmos committed by Satan himself (Ezek. 28:12–17; *cf.* 2 Peter 2:4; 1 John 3:8). Since his temptation of Adam and Eve to sin against God in the garden (Gen. 3:1–6), Satan, along with his demon hordes, has conducted a guerilla warfare campaign to deceive and enslave men and women in his kingdom of darkness. Mankind's only hope is therefore in God's redeeming grace, "For He rescued us from the domain of darkness, and transferred us to the kingdom of His beloved Son, in whom we have redemption, the forgiveness of sins" (Col. 1:13–14); causing us to turn "from darkness to light and from the dominion of Satan to God" (Acts 26:18).

The anti-God world system God allows Satan to temporarily control consists of human beings who are willing subjects of his rule that is mediated in his kingdom by "rulers . . . world forces of this darkness [and] the spiritual forces of wickedness in the heavenly places" (Eph. 6:12). History is replete with examples of men and women who wittingly and unwittingly do his bidding. Together, they rebel against the Most High God. For this reason, God has cursed His creation. "For the creation was subjected to futility, not of its own will, but because of Him who subjected it, in hope that the creation itself also will be set free from its slavery to corruption into the freedom of the glory of the children of God" (Rom. 8:20–21). John MacArthur has rightly stated:

> The universal kingdom is suffering the effects of rebellion. It is cursed because of sin, both that of the human race, and of Satan and the demons. That curse has stained it both spiritually and physically. As a result, what scientists call the second law of thermodynamics is operating, and the universe is running down, heading toward its disastrous dissolution when "the heavens will be destroyed by burning, and the elements will melt with intense heat" (2 Peter 3:12)! Spiritually, Satan and his demon hosts, along with the fallen human race, persist in foolishly and futilely attempting to thwart the kingdom purposes of almighty God.[7]

Who Is Satan?

The various names and titles found in Scripture betray Satan's character and the nature of his kingdom, some of which include:

- Accuser of our brethren (Rev. 12:10)
- Adversary (1 Peter 5:8)
- Angel of the bottomless pit (Rev. 9:11)
- Belial (2 Cor. 6:15)
- Distressing spirit (1 Sam. 16:14)
- Dragon (Rev. 20:2)

7   John MacArthur, *The MacArthur New Testament Commentary: Luke 11–17* (Chicago, Illinois: Moody Publishers, 2013), 399.

- Enemy (Matt. 13:39)
- Father of lies (John 8:44)
- Liar (John 8:44)
- Lying spirit (1 Kings 22:22)
- Murderer (John 8:44)
- Prince of the power of the air (Eph. 2:2)
- Ruler of the darkness of this world (Eph. 6:12)
- Ruler of the demons (Matt. 12:24)
- Ruler of this world (John 14:30)
- Satan (1 Chron. 12:1; Job 1:6)
- Serpent (Gen. 3:4, 13–14; 2 Cor. 11:3)
- Spirit who works in the sons of disobedience (Eph. 2:2)
- Tempter (Matt. 4:3)
- The god of this age (2 Cor. 4:4)
- Wicked one (Matt. 13:19)

Jesus said unbelievers "are of [their] father the devil . . ." and "want to do the desires of [their] father" who "was a murderer from the beginning, and does not stand in the truth because there is no truth in him" (John 8:44). Paul said they "walk in the futility of their mind, being darkened in their understanding, excluded from the life of God, because of the ignorance that is in them, because of the of the hardness of their heart; and they, having become callous, have given themselves over to sensuality, for the practice of every kind of impurity with greediness" (Eph. 4:17–19)—a perfect description of America today. Our nation is characterized by lawlessness, darkness, and spiritual death, in contrast to believers who are characterized by righteousness, light, and spiritual life (2 Cor. 6:14–16).

"Coexist"

Christians and non-Christians coexist on this planet physically, but not spiritually. You might say we live in two different worlds. This is why we often hear people spitefully say, "These Christians are from another planet!" And at one level, they're right. Jesus said, "They are not of the world, even as I am not of the world" (John 17:14). In fact, we guard ourselves from being "conformed to this world" (Rom. 12:2). Why? because it is ruled by Satan (John 14:30) and it has no appeal to us, "for if anyone loves the world, the love of the Father is not in him" (1 John 2:15). We are people of another realm and our allegiance is to another King. And by the inspired Scriptures and personal experience, we know "the whole world lies in the power of the evil one" (1 John 5:19) and is under the power of "Satan, who deceives the whole world" (Rev. 12:9).

But unbelievers love this sin-cursed world—a world "that is passing away" (1 John 2:17), a world characterized by "the lust of the flesh and the lust of the eyes and the boastful pride of life" (1 John 2:16). The reason they love this world is because—and I say this with utmost regret and compassion—*they are citizens of Satan's kingdom*, "slaves to impurity and to lawlessness, resulting in *further* lawlessness" (Rom. 6:19). G. C. Trench described the contemporary beliefs and values that make up the moral environment of our world as,

> That floating mass of thoughts, opinions, maxims, specula-
> tions, hopes, impulses, aims, aspirations, at any time current
> in the world which it may be impossible to seize and accu-
> rately define, but which constitute a most real and effective
> power, being the moral or immoral atmosphere which in ev-
> ery moment of our lives we inhale, again inevitable to exhale.[8]

This is why at a most fundamental spiritual and moral level, true Christians have nothing in common with unbelievers (which includes the vast majority of Americans) and are commanded to never be bound together with them in any spiritual, religious endeavor (2 Cor. 6:14–18). This is why we cannot "COEXIST" with other religions in some unified global spirituality as the bumper sticker suggests (I cringe every time I see it and pray for the poor individual who proudly and foolishly affirms such deception). Bottom line: *We are not of this world.* Jesus said, "If you were of the world, the world would love its own; but because you are not of the world, but I chose you out of the world, because of this the world hates you" (John 15:19).

8 G. C. Trench, *Synonyms of the New Testament*, (Grand Rapids, Michigan: Eerdmans, 1973), 217–18.

The Christian's Allegiance

The vast majority of Americans simply cannot grasp the fact that as Christians we are citizens of another kingdom and our allegiance is to King Jesus. This is why the neo-Marxist ideologies of the progressive left in America intend to marginalize and eventually outlaw biblical Christianity. The two are utterly incompatible at every level. Christians are loyal to Christ, not to the state. God is our moral authority, not man. As the apostle stated, "Our citizenship is in heaven, from which also we eagerly wait for a Savior, the Lord Jesus Christ; who will transform the body of our humble state into conformity with the body of His glory, by the exertion of the power that He has even to subject all things to Himself" (Phil. 3:20). Therefore, in obedience to our King's command, we pray for the coming of the kingdom so His will can be done on earth as it is in heaven (Matt. 6:10). And God's will is always contrary to Satan's will.

This is why America hates *biblical* Christianity. This is why so many people scoff at the gospel and do things so exceedingly immoral and wicked. This is why they see nothing wrong with things like abortion and try so desperately to force everyone to embrace the LGBTQ agenda. And this is why they violently resent being lovingly warned—often at the risk of injury—that those who practice these things will never inherit the kingdom of God (1 Cor. 6:9–10). But, for the sake of the gospel, they need our *compassion*— not our *contempt*. As Christians, we must remember that were it not for God's grace, we would be among them. Regrettably, they remain prisoners in the kingdom of Satan, because "the god of this world has blinded the minds of the unbelieving, that they might not see the light of the gospel of the glory of Christ, who is the image of God" (2 Cor. 4:4).

What About You?

To which kingdom do you belong? The *kingdom of God* accessed by repentant faith in the Lord Jesus Christ, or the *kingdom of Satan* that is opposed to Him and seeks your eternal destruction? This is the question I earnestly ask you to consider. Do not be deceived:

one day you will bow before King Jesus either in *humble adoration* or *defiant trepidation*. If the former, you will hear Him say, "Well done, good and faithful slave . . . enter into the joy of your master" (Matt. 25:22), but if the latter, you will hear the dreadful sentence, "Throw out the worthless slave into the outer darkness; in that place there will be weeping and gnashing of teeth" (v. 30). Your response to the King's provision of saving grace set forth in the gospel of God will determine your destiny.

And what about you, Christian reader? Are you staggering under the weight of mounting persecution? Has your faith grown cold? Has your hope yielded to apathy? Have you given up on finding joy in sorrow and strength in weakness? Let me offer you one final word of encouragement that is sure to satisfy your soul.

Concluding Words of Encouragement

Daniel 2 records Daniel's interpretation of Nebuchadnezzar's terrifying dream of an immense Colossus representing a succession of world empires. There God revealed the consecutive empires that would dominate the world in the future, starting with the Babylonian empire ruled by Nebuchadnezzar (the golden head), that would eventually fall to the Medo-Persian empire (the silver torso), that would then be conquered by Alexander's Greek empire (the abdomen and legs of bronze), that would later be crushed by the Roman empire (the legs of iron). This was followed by another kingdom *related* to the iron kingdom of Rome, but not nearly as stable since its feet were of a mixture of iron and clay, what is believed to be a reference to a final and future form of the fourth kingdom (Rome) that will consist of a coalition of nations.

But the most exciting aspect of the prophetic dream pertains to God's final kingdom pictured as a "stone" that "was cut out without hands" and strikes the feet of the massive image so that it becomes "a great mountain that fills the whole earth." The "stone" is a reference to the Messiah (*cf.* Ps. 118:22, 23; Isa. 28:16; Rom. 9:33; 1 Peter 2:6; especially Luke 20:18) and the "great mountain" pictures God's invincible and all-encompassing kingdom that utterly annihilates all the prevailing Gentile powers on earth who are part of *Satan's kingdom*.

This is what I long for! This is what every man and woman who bows the knee to King Jesus longs for. Thankfully, God's *universal kingdom* will ultimately prevail over *Satan's kingdom* of darkness. The usurper will be forever deposed, and the universe will be forever purged from sin. For this reason, we read in Daniel 7:14 that "... to Him was given dominion, glory and a kingdom, that all the peoples, nations and men of every language might serve Him. His dominion is an everlasting dominion which will not pass away; and His kingdom is one which will not be destroyed."

In light of these divine certainties, with the apostle Paul every true Christian can enthusiastically declare: "Now to the King eternal, immortal, invisible, the only God, be honor and glory forever and ever. Amen" (1 Tim. 1:17). I trust this is the sincere sentiment of your heart.

2

· · · · · · · · · · · ·

The Christian's Affection

A Clash of Worldviews

The world is passing away, and also its lusts;
but the one who does the will of God lives forever.

1 John 2:17

The United States Declaration of Independence states: "We hold these truths to be self-evident, that all men are created equal, that they are endowed by their Creator with certain unalienable Rights, that among these are Life, Liberty and the Pursuit of Happiness." Our founders believed that these three unalienable rights were to be protected by government. Obviously, they were not. As a result, thirteen American colonies revolted against Great Britain and formed a new nation—the United States of America.

Ever since that Declaration was written, our country has tried to achieve those goals—often referred to as "the American Dream"—despite differing opinions on how to attain them. This can be seen in the disparate views of the Republican and Democratic National Parties that manifest such acrimonious division in the country today.

Capitalism or Democratic Socialism: The Dramatic Differences

At a most fundamental level, in order to protect the unalienable rights of "Life, Liberty and the Pursuit of Happiness," the Republican National Party advocates for limited government and personal responsibility, which is at the heart of capitalism. The moral doctrine of individualism, where each individual is regarded as an end in oneself and not as a slave for the ends of others, is held sacred. The right to pursue and achieve happiness in life belongs solely to the individual to live as he or she pleases, as long as it does not violate the rights of others. For the capitalist, a proper government does not have the right to force individuals to give up their property or freedoms for the sake of others they deem oppressed, and the constitution protects against public officials who seek to use their political power to force their will on citizens.

On the other hand, the Democratic National Party believes in a socially owned economy requiring broad government control to promote egalitarianism, which is at the heart of Democratic Socialism. They believe individualism (inherent in capitalism) empowers the rich to oppress the poor in a white, patriarchal society where white people benefit from power and privilege that other disenfranchised groups do not possess. This is extremely problematic, however, since our country was founded upon Judeo-Christian ethics inscribed in the Constitution (which happened to be written by white men) that holds sacred the doctrine of individualism. Therefore, carried to its logical end, many of the egalitarian goals of Democratic Socialism are at legal loggerheads with the Constitution as written.

Not only that, since many of their moral values violate God's righteous standards recorded in Scripture—the Christian's spiritual and moral authority—they are also at odds with Christ's true church. Bottom line: for the Democratic Socialist, the "unalienable rights of Life, Liberty, and the Pursuit of Happiness" require the abolition of capitalism, the Constitution, and biblical Christianity. The extreme and even corrupt measures they employ to prevent originalist judges from being appointed to the Supreme Court betray their intentions.

The proponents of this thinking envision an egalitarian utopia that requires all social, gender, economic, and political inequities (as they define them) to be eradicated. Practically speaking, this means the *government* must be in charge of defining what is fair and unfair. The *government* must determine what is morally and socially acceptable. Then the *government* must equally distribute wealth, opportunities, outcomes, and privileges for the citizens—a subjective and arbitrary system of justice based solely upon the moral authority of men and women, not God.

Obviously, conservatives who embrace capitalism—and Bible-believing Christians—believe this political ideology will not only infringe upon the rights of those the state deems morally and socially unacceptable and therefore oppressive, but that it will also continue an aggressive "cancel culture" and legal campaign to silence all who oppose them—and especially those people who oppose a woman's right to dismember her inconvenient baby in her womb, those who find the LGBTQ agenda morally reprehensible, and those who believe gender is based upon biology rather than personal preference.

This can be seen in the so-called *Equality Act*, a proposed bill that would add "sexual orientation" and "gender identity" as protected classes under federal civil rights law. This will be a powerful legal tool they will use to force their values on others if passed into law. The Heritage Foundation explains this danger:

> Where the original Civil Rights Act of 1964 furthered equality by ensuring that African-Americans had equal access to public accommodations and material goods, the Equality Act would further *inequality* by penalizing everyday Americans for their beliefs about marriage and biological sex. Similar sexual orientation and gender identity laws at the state and local level have already been used in this way. . . . The Equality Act would force employers and workers to conform to new sexual norms or else lose their businesses and jobs. . . . [It] would force hospitals and insurers to provide and pay for these therapies against any moral or medical objections. . . . [It] would politicize medicine by forcing professionals to act against their best medical judgment and provide transition-affirming therapies. [It] would ultimately harm families by normalizing hormonal and surgical intervention for gender dysphoric children as well as ideological "education" in schools and other public venues. . . . [It] would put parental rights to make decisions about their children's medical treatment and education at risk . . . [It] would ultimately lead to the erasure of women by dismantling sex-specific facilities, sports, and other female-only spaces. . . . [It] would also hurt charities, volunteers, and the populations they serve. . . . A federal sexual orientation and gender identity law would empower the government to interfere in how regular Americans think, speak, and act at home, at school, at work and at play. Any bill promoting such authoritarianism is a danger to our freedoms.[9]

A Transcendent Christian Worldview

In stark contrast to the liberal ideologies and policies of Democratic Socialism, and even in contrast to many of the conservative Republican positions, there exists another worldview that is so far removed from American thought that it is considered by most

---

9 https://www.heritage.org/gender/heritage-explains/the-equality-act

to be utterly bizarre, the delusional musings of religious fools not tethered to reality. This, of course, is a reference to biblical Christianity.

Because of the transforming power of the gospel, we love God supremely—the foremost commandment (Matt. 22:37-38). We love His Word and joyfully obey it (John 14:23). Therefore, mature and faithful Christians have no love for this present world or the things in it that will all pass away (1 John 2:15-17). "We look not at the things which are seen, but at the things which are not seen; for the things which are seen are temporal, but the things which are not seen are eternal" (2 Cor. 4:18). "Our citizenship is heaven, from which also we eagerly wait for a Savior, the Lord Jesus Christ; who will transform the body of our humble state into conformity with the body of His glory, by the exertion of the power that He has even to subject all things to Himself" (Phil. 3:20).

As explained in chapter one, the Christian belongs to the *Kingdom of God* and views the world in which we currently reside as *Satan's kingdom*. Not only that—we can't wait for our glorious King to come and take us out of this sin-cursed realm where the "unalienable Rights [of] Life, Liberty, and the Pursuit of Happiness" are constantly threatened and can never be fully realized. We put no confidence in the wisdom of man, political parties, or human government (although we willingly submit to it as God has commanded [Rom. 13:13:1-7]). The Christian's only hope is in God's redeeming grace, "For He rescued us from the domain of darkness, and transferred us to the kingdom of His beloved Son, in whom we have redemption, the forgiveness of sins" (Col. 1:13-14), causing us to turn "from darkness to light and from the dominion of Satan to God" (Acts 26:18).

Neither Republicans nor Democrats can identify with any of this, nor can most Americans. In fact, most people find these fundamentals of the Christian faith to be quite preposterous, and even consider us to be hateful and bigoted when we agree with God's Word and obey His will on matters that are contrary to the prevailing social and moral values of our culture. So for the Christian, neither political party nor government can provide the peace and prosperity every American wants. The "American Dream" is just that—*a dream*; a fantasy with only limited fulfillment in this life—but one that envisions a future realm of heavenly bliss. One only, the "Prince of Peace" who will bring "the increase of His government and peace" can establish through His justice by His judgment (Isa. 9:7); only "The zeal of the LORD of hosts will accomplish this" (v. 8).

The Christian Utopia

In light of all this, America continues to develop a growing resentment for biblical Christianity—not only because we believe ours is the only true religion, but also because of our divergent worldview on how to achieve utopia on earth. Our position is simply too extreme and out of touch with the culture, not to mention too offensive to those who differ. While conservative Republicans have their view and Liberal Democrats have theirs, both are ultimately at odds with Christian theology.

Think about it very practically. Most Americans in both political parties live for this world, whereas Christians live for heaven. Their priority is the "pursuit of Life, Liberty, and ... Happiness"; our pursuit is the glory of God. They live for this life only; we live for eternity. They set their affections on the things of the earth; we set our affections on things above. They lay up treasures on earth; we lay up treasures in heaven. They consider this world their home; we consider ourselves strangers in it. They obsess over preserving the planet; we believe God will destroy it and recreate it. They obey the ever-changing morality of a sin-cursed culture; we obey the never-changing laws of an infinitely holy God. They believe people can achieve utopia on earth; we believe God alone can bring in everlasting righteousness, peace, and prosperity. Can there be any greater disparities in worldviews than these few examples? I think not.

Imagine the stunned reaction of the masses if a Christian political candidate announced publicly that at a most fundamental level he or she believed

> the grace of God has appeared, bringing salvation to all men, instructing us to deny ungodliness and worldly desires and to live sensibly, righteously and godly in the present age,

> looking for the blessed hope and the appearing of the glory
> of our great God and Savior, Christ Jesus, who gave Himself
> for us to redeem us from every lawless deed, and to puri-
> fy for Himself a people for His own possession, zealous for
> good deeds.
> (Titus 2:11–14)

And it is the Christian's certainty of this eternal destiny that provides the theological lens through which we view all of life, including politics. We know that whomever God allows to be placed in authority over us, no matter how wicked, His sovereign purposes will ultimately be accomplished (Isa. 46:10).

As mentioned in chapter one, many Christians believe (as I do) that God will judge the earth in a special tribulation period (Dan. 9:24–27; Matt. 24–25; Rev. 6–18) prior to His physical return to earth to establish a glorious millennial kingdom (Rev. 20) where He will reign on renovated earth with His saints after this present age and before the eternal state. This will be the utopia people have always dreamed of. It will be a time of prosperity, righteousness, peace, and international harmony among the nations (Matt. 19:28; Isa. 2:2–4; 11; 65:17–25); a time when all covenant promises made to Israel, both spiritual and physical, will be fulfilled and all nations will enjoy the same blessings with them (Isa. 19:16–25). Others believe the millennial kingdom reign of Christ refers to Jesus' current rule from heaven along with His perfected saints; yet others believe it refers to Jesus reigning in the hearts of believers; and there are others who believe in variations of both views.

Nevertheless, all Christians agree that Jesus Christ is "KING OF KINGS, AND LORD OF LORDS" (Rev. 19:16) and will one day rule over a new heaven and a new earth (21:1). One day the curse will be lifted; sin, Satan, and death defeated at the cross will be forever removed (22:3) and everyone who has been washed in the blood of the Lamb "will see His face" (22:3–4) and "will reign forever and ever" with Him (22:5). These eschatological promises shape everything we think and do. They motivate us to live for Christ, not for people. We live in light of eternity, not for this life only. The certainties of our salvation and heavenly destiny cause us to say with the apostle John, "Come, Lord Jesus!" (Rev. 22:20). But until He does, we exhibit our new life in the risen Christ by obeying the apostle Paul's command recorded in Colossians 3:1-4:

> Therefore if you have been raised up with Christ, keep seeking the things above, where Christ is, seated at the right hand of God. Set your mind on the things above, not on the things that are on earth. For you have died and your life is hidden with Christ in God. When Christ, who is our life, is revealed, then you also will be revealed with Him in glory.

Everyone Has a Theology—Including Unbelievers

When we look at the divergent worldviews expressed in the dominant political parties in America and contrast them with those of the biblical Christian, we see how theology—that is, Bible teaching—shapes everyone's thinking. For example, the founding of the United States was largely a product of Protestant Reformation theology in that many of the early immigrants were seeking religious freedom in the new land. We also know the Constitution was written from a Judeo-Christian theological framework. To be sure, all people have underlying theological assumptions that instruct their thinking. Whether atheist, deist, agnostic, or theist, everyone has a theology.

But authentic Christians assert there is only one correct theology that forms the very basis of Christianity: *that which can only be derived from God's supernatural self-disclosure recorded in Scripture.* As God's image bearers created by Him and for Him, we are, according to Jesus, to live only by "that [which] proceeds out of the mouth of God" (Matt. 4:4). And His words are only to be found in the canonical Scriptures of the Old and New Testaments of the Bible, the only basis of Christian theology. There God reveals Himself as the one living and true God, perfect in all His attributes, one in essence, eternally existing in three Persons—Father, Son, and Holy Spirit—each deserving worship and obedience. There He discloses His unfathomable and infinite perfections as the Creator, Sustainer, Redeemer, and Consummator of all things; the infinitely holy and sovereign God of the universe who has revealed Himself in creation, Scripture, and in the person and work of His Son, the Lord Jesus Christ, the only means by which sinners can be saved and have eternal life.

Of course, postmodern and post-Christian America is radically opposed to this view. People think of it as nothing more than superstitious, archaic, and bigoted religious dogmatism. For most individuals, there is no standard of absolute moral truth. Truth is determined by what feels right subjectively in a given circumstance, or what the collective whole of society has agreed is morally and socially acceptable. For them, religious dogma and supernaturalism are all based on superstition and myths, but human reason and inherent goodness can be trusted to make proper ethical and moral decisions. So, they think that someone can achieve self-fulfillment without any belief in God whatsoever, if that is his or her preference. This, of course, is at the heart of the philosophy known as *secular humanism*—the prevailing way of thinking in America. A close second would be *practical atheism*—regardless of religious affiliation—in which people live as if there is no God, even if they claim otherwise.

It is important to understand, however, that these wrong theologies are consistent with God's warnings about the schemes of Satan, the "father of lies" (John 8:44), the "ruler of this world" (John 14:30), "the god of this world [who] has blinded the minds of the unbelieving so that they might not see the light of the gospel of the glory of Christ, who is the image of God" (2 Cor. 4:4). Through the use of false teachers who are either witting or unwitting purveyors of "doctrines of demons" (1 Tim. 4:1), Satan deceives both believers and nonbelievers alike. And it is this kind of satanic deception in the realm of theology that he has used to not only divide America politically and morally, but also to fuel a growing hostility toward Christians. The theology of former president Barack Obama and the policies he embraces (along with most on the liberal left) illustrate how satanic theologies manifest themselves in contemporary America and why so many people hate biblical Christianity.

Black Liberation Theology

I first heard of Barack Obama when he was a presidential candidate. Knowing nothing about him, I decided to investigate his background. As a shepherd of God's people, responsible for protecting my flock, I first wanted to know about his theology, especially since he courted evangelicals and emphasized how his Christian faith influenced his policies. I quickly discovered that he belonged to the Trinity United Church of Christ in Chicago for twenty years—a controversial church he later severed ties with during his campaign.

Since this was an apostate church that preached a false gospel rooted in *Black Liberation Theology* (BLT), I thought to myself, "Oh my, this guy will never get elected if people find out what he believes." I remember telling folks, "This man attends a Black Liberation Theology church. This is the same theology of the socialist Nicaraguan Sandinistas of the 1960s, modeled after the Cuban revolution. There's no way he'll get elected." My, was I ever wrong! But sadly, most Americans never learned about his theology, and many who did, just didn't care. Most Americans have no biblical, theological discernment, and even to this day have no understanding of *Black Liberation Theology*.

In an article by Barbara Hagerty entitled, *A Closer Look at Black Liberation Theology* and published by Nashville Public Radio (heard on *All Things Considered*) it is noted that: "Black liberation theology originated on July 31, 1966, when 51 black pastors bought a full page ad in the New York Times and demanded a more aggressive approach to eradicating racism...echo[ing] the demands of the black power movement."[10]

At a most basic level, BLT believes Jesus is a savior to liberate black people from the bondage of white people, not from the bondage of sin. Jesus is not the Lamb of God who takes away the sins of the world (John 1:29); He was a revolutionary who sought to free His people from white, Roman bondage. It's a theology that centers on *victimhood* and *oppression*. Salvation is all about equality and social justice. As a result, the mission of the church is to effect political change. It's essentially a religious version of

---

10   https://www.npr.org/templates/story/story.php?storyId=88512189

Marxism. The experience of oppression—not Scripture—is their authority. It's a man-centered—not a God-centered—theology, and it's humanistic and pragmatic to the core. It's all about people and their needs, not God and His glory.

This can be seen in the rhetoric of one of Obama's controversial pastors, Jeremiah Wright, who said, "Jesus was a poor, black man who lived in a country and who lived in a culture that was controlled by rich white people. The Romans were Italian—which means they were Europeans, which means they were white—and the Romans ran everything in Jesus' country."[11] Wright's hatred for white people is consistent with his theology; it can be seen in one of his racist rants where he said "There will be no peace in America until whites begin to hate their whiteness."[12]

James Cone, one of the leading theological voices in the BLT movement, espouses the same racist heresy. In his 1970 book, *A Black Theology of Liberation*, Cone advanced the notion of a deity that sided with blacks, and against whites:

> Black theology refuses to accept a God who is not identified totally with the goals of the Black community. If God is not for us and against White people, then he is a murderer, and we had better kill him. The task of Black theology is to kill Gods who do not belong to the Black community . . . Black theology will accept only the love of God which participates in the destruction of the White enemy. What we need is the divine love as expressed in Black Power, which is the power of Black people to destroy their oppressors here and now by any means at their disposal. Unless God is participating in this holy activity, we must reject his love.[13]

This means the message of the gospel is essentially *Black Power*. Cone made this clear when he said, "It is my thesis . . . that Black Power, even in its most radical expression, is not the antithesis of Christianity, nor is it a heretical idea to be tolerated

---

11   https://www.azquotes.com/author/15967-Jeremiah_Wright

12   https://100percentfedup.com/shocking-evidence-shows-obama-heart-violent-blacklivesmatter-cop-killing-anti-white-movement/

13   https://www.discoverthenetworks.org/individuals/james-cone/

with painful forbearance. It is, rather, Christ's central message."[14] He defines *Black Power* as "the complete emancipation of black people from white oppression by whatever means Black people deem necessary."[15] Similarly and more forcefully, Hayward Henry (author of *Toward a Religion of Revolution*) says, "Black Power is not the antithesis of Christianity. It is Christianity."[16]

Black Lives Matter and Critical Race Theory

The parallels between BLT, the *Black Nationalist* ideas and race-based theology of *Nation of Islam* (Louis Farrakhan) are undeniable. But they also help us see how Barack Obama's theology provided fertile soil for the formation of the BLM movement to flourish. Andre Johnson, who reviewed James Cone's book, *Black Theology and Black Power*, offered this insightful analysis:

> Proponents of Black Lives Matter (BLM) use the same language today. Created in 2012, BLM grounds itself in the "experiences of Black people who actively resist de-humanization." BLM "is an affirmation of Black folks' humanity, [their] contributions to this society, and [their] resilience in the face of deadly oppression." BLM challenges the "very foundations upon which Americans claim their democracy is built: that we are all created equal, that all are equally entitled to life, liberty, and the pursuit of happiness" (Amanda Nell Edgar and Andre E. Johnson, *The Struggle Over Black Lives Matter and All Lives Matter,* Lexington Books, 2018).[17]

Alicia Garza, one of three militant feminists and self-proclaimed Marxists that founded BLM, detailed the philosophy behind the organization in her October 2014 article titled, *A Herstory of the #BlackLivesMatter Movement*. She writes:

> Black Lives Matter is a unique contribution that goes beyond extrajudicial killings of Black people by police and vigilan-

---

14 https://www.monergism.com/thethreshold/sdg/blackliberation.html
15 https://readingreligion.org/books/black-theology-and-black-power
16 https://www.monergism.com/thethreshold/sdg/blackliberation.html
17 https://readingreligion.org/books/black-theology-and-black-power

tes. It goes beyond the narrow nationalism that can be prevalent within some Black communities, which merely call on Black people to love Black, live Black and buy Black, keeping straight cis Black men in the front of the movement while our sisters, queer and trans and disabled folk take up roles in the background or not at all. Black Lives Matter affirms the lives of Black queer and trans folks, disabled folks, Black-undocumented folks, folks with records, women and all Black lives along the gender spectrum. It centers those that have been marginalized within Black liberation movements. It is a tactic to (re)build the Black liberation movement.[18]

This same philosophy, rooted in the satanically inspired heresies of BLT and the counterfeit gospel it espouses, is also at the heart of *Critical Race Theory* (CRT).

The view that the law and legal institutions are inherently racist and that race itself, instead of being biologically grounded and natural, is a socially constructed concept that is used by white people to further their economic and political interests at the expense of people of colour. According to critical race theory (CRT), racial inequality emerges from the social, economic, and legal differences that white people create between "races" to maintain elite white interests in labour markets and politics, giving rise to poverty and criminality in many minority communities.[19]

In Columbia, Missouri, on October 30, 2008, on the cusp of his historic presidential election, Barack Obama made a bold statement: "We are five days away from fundamentally transforming the United States of America." And during his two-term presidency, he fulfilled his promise primarily in the sphere of cultural morality. It should be no surprise that in 2011, then president Barack Obama issued an executive order that required all federal agencies, government workers, even our military, "to promote diversity and inclusion" through mandated training courses. What sounds innocent was in fact a sophisticated scheme to indoctrinate federal officials with a virulent strain of identity politics rooted CRT, an extension of BLT that was so heavily

---

18   https://100percentfedup.com/shocking-evidence-shows-obama-heart-violent-blacklivesmatter-cop-killing-anti-white-movement/

19   https://www.britannica.com/topic/critical-race-theory

promoted by the Obama Administration and continues to enjoy such a high priority in the platform of the Democratic Party. Frustrated with the relentless accusations of systemic racism and white privilege, combined with the rampaging violence and lawlessness of ANTIFA and BLM, conservative lawmakers knew they had to do something to prevent total anarchy. And the snake's head was the divisive, anti-American propaganda propagated by CRT in the "training" of government workers. As a result, President Donald Trump issued an order to "cease and desist from using taxpayer dollars" for the dissemination of CRT. The order directed federal agencies to begin the process of identifying and eliminating "all contracts or other agency spending related to any training on 'critical race theory,' 'white privilege,' or any other training or propaganda effort that teaches or suggests either (1) that the United States is an inherently racist or evil country or (2) that any race or ethnicity is inherently racist or evil."[20]

A False Gospel Brings Destruction and Sends People to Hell

This is what happens when a nation rejects God's revelation of Himself and mocks His gospel invitation. This is what happens when a nation has no fear of God and refuses to love Him supremely so it can be empowered to love others as themselves (Matt. 22:37–39). This is where satanic deception will lead. This is what happens when the true gospel is replaced by "another gospel"—something so horrible that it must be met with this warning: "But even if we, or an angel from heaven, should preach to you a gospel contrary to what we have preached to you, he is to be accursed!" (Gal. 1:8). Deception is deadly, especially as it relates to the gospel. And as we witness on a daily basis, a false gospel will destroy a nation.

Of course, as Christians, we are opposed to any form of racism, hatred, inequity, and injustice—problems that have always existed in this sin-cursed world and that will continue to exist until the curse is lifted. But there's a far greater problem than *social injustice* (much of which is grossly exaggerated and demonstrably

---

20   https://www.whitehouse.gov/wp-content/uploads/2020/09/M-20-34.pdf

false). *The greatest problem is the need for sinful people to be reconciled to a holy God.* By nature, however, man sees himself as being *deprived,* not *depraved.* But man is a sinner by nature; *sin is simply an innate inability to conform to the moral character and desires of God.* Indeed, "sin is lawlessness" (1 John 3:4), which is not only a failure to obey God's moral law, *but living as if it does not exist.* It is a violation of the greatest commandment to love the Lord our God supremely. God has made it clear that "all have sinned and fall short of the glory of God" (Rom. 3:23) and "the wages of sin is death, but the free gift of God is eternal life in Christ Jesus our Lord" (Rom. 6:23). And Jesus declared, "He who believes in the Son has eternal life; but he who does not obey the Son will not see life, but the wrath of God abides on him" (John 3:36). However, America rejects these divine truths. Worse yet, it hates those who believe them, live them, and proclaim them.

Nevertheless the message people need to hear today is not *how to be delivered from the social injustice of man but how to be delivered from the righteous justice of God.* Yet the deceptive theologies that form the basis of BLT, BLM, and CRT ignore and despise this most basic gospel truth. The result will only end in further division, violence, persecution of Christians, and ultimately divine judgment.

How the Bible Views Social Justice

An excellent summary of how biblical theology should inform our thinking as it relates to the clash of worldviews that are wreaking havoc in America can be found in *The Statement on Social Justice and the Gospel*[21] that reads in part as follows:

> In view of questionable sociological, psychological, and po-
> litical theories presently permeating our culture and mak-
> ing inroads into Christ's church, we wish to clarify certain
> key Christian doctrines and ethical principles prescribed in
> God's Word. Clarity on these issues will fortify believers and
> churches to withstand an onslaught of dangerous and false
> teachings that threaten the gospel, misrepresent Scripture,
> and lead people away from the grace of God in Jesus Christ.

---

21 https://statementonsocialjustice.com

Specifically, we are deeply concerned that values borrowed from secular culture are currently undermining Scripture in the areas of race and ethnicity, manhood and womanhood, and human sexuality. The Bible's teaching on each of these subjects is being challenged under the broad and somewhat nebulous rubric of concern for "social justice." If the doctrines of God's Word are not uncompromisingly reasserted and defended at these points, there is every reason to anticipate that these dangerous ideas and corrupted moral values will spread their influence into other realms of biblical doctrines and principles.

We submit these affirmations and denials for public consideration, not with any pretense of ecclesiastical authority, but with an urgency that is mixed with deep joy and sincere sorrow. The rapidity with which these deadly ideas have spread from the culture at large into churches and Christian organizations—including some that are evangelical and Reformed—necessitates the issuing of this statement now.

THE STATEMENT ON SOCIAL JUSTICE AND THE GOSPEL

I: Scripture

WE AFFIRM that the Bible is God's Word, breathed out by him. It is inerrant, infallible, and the final authority for determining what is true (what we must believe) and what is right (how we must live). All truth claims and ethical standards must be tested by God's final Word, which is Scripture alone.

WE DENY that Christian belief, character, or conduct can be dictated by any other authority, and we deny that the postmodern ideologies derived from intersectionality, radical feminism, and critical race theory are consistent with biblical teaching. We further deny that competency to teach on any biblical issue comes from any qualification for spiritual people other than clear understanding and simple communication of what is revealed in Scripture.

SCRIPTURE: Genesis 2:18–25; Psalm 19:7–10; 1 Corinthians 2:14–15; Ephesians 5:22–33; 2 Timothy 3:16–4:5; Hebrews 4:12; 13:4; 1 Peter 1:25; 2 Peter 1:19–21

II: Imago Dei

WE AFFIRM that God created every person equally in his own image. As divine image-bearers, all people have inestimable value and dignity before God and deserve honor, respect and protection. Everyone has been created by God and for God.

WE DENY that God-given roles, socioeconomic status, ethnicity, religion, sex or physical condition or any other property of a person either negates or contributes to that individual's worth as an image-bearer of God.

SCRIPTURE: Genesis 1:26–30; 2:18–22; 9:6; 2 Corinthians 5:17; Colossians 1:21–22

III: Justice

WE AFFIRM that since he is holy, righteous, and just, God requires those who bear his image to live justly in the world. This includes showing appropriate respect to every person and giving to each one what he or she is due. We affirm that societies must establish laws to correct injustices that have been imposed through cultural prejudice.

WE DENY that true justice can be culturally defined or that standards of justice that are merely socially constructed can be imposed with the same authority as those that are derived from Scripture. We further deny that Christians can live justly in the world under any principles other than the biblical standard of righteousness. Relativism, socially-constructed standards of truth or morality, and notions of virtue and vice that are constantly in flux cannot result in authentic justice.

SCRIPTURE: Genesis 18:19; Isaiah 61:8; Micah 6:8; Matthew 5:17–19; Romans 3:31

IV: God's Law

WE AFFIRM that God's law, as summarized in the ten commandments, more succinctly summarized in the two great commandments, and manifested in Jesus Christ, is the only standard of unchanging righteousness. Violation of that law is what constitutes sin.

WE DENY that any obligation that does not arise from God's commandments can be legitimately imposed on Christians as a prescription for righteous living. We further deny the legitimacy of any charge of sin or call to repentance that does not arise from a violation of God's commandments.

SCRIPTURE: Deuteronomy 10:4; Romans 6:14, 10:5; Galatians 2:16, 3:10, 12; Colossians 2:14– 17; Hebrews 10:1

V: Sin

WE AFFIRM that all people are connected to Adam both naturally and federally. Therefore, because of original sin everyone is born under the curse of God's law and all break his commandments through sin. There is no difference in the condition of sinners due to age, ethnicity, or sex. All are depraved in all their faculties and all stand condemned before God's law. All human relationships, systems, and institutions have been affected by sin.

WE DENY that, other than the previously stated connection to Adam, any person is morally culpable for another person's sin. Although families, groups, and nations can sin collectively, and cultures can be predisposed to particular sins, subsequent generations share the collective guilt of their ancestors only if they approve and embrace (or attempt to justify) those sins. Before God each person must repent and confess his or her own sins in order to receive forgiveness. We further deny that one's ethnicity establishes any necessary connection to any particular sin.

SCRIPTURE: Genesis 2:16, 17, 3:12,13–15; Proverbs 29:18; Isaiah 25:7, 60:2–3; Jeremiah 31:27–34; Ezekiel 18:1–9, 14–18; Matthew 23:29–36; Romans 1:16–17, 3:23, 5:12, 10:14–17; 1 Corinthians 15:3–11; 2 Corinthians 11:3; Galatians 1:6–9; Titus 1:12, 13; Revelation 13:8

VI: Gospel

WE AFFIRM that the gospel is the divinely-revealed message concerning the person and work of Jesus Christ—especially his virgin birth, righteous life, substitutionary sacrifice, atoning death, and bodily resurrection—revealing who he is and what he has done with the promise that he will save anyone and everyone who turns from sin by trusting him as Lord.

WE DENY that anything else, whether works to be performed or opinions to be held, can be added to the gospel without perverting it into another gospel. This also means that implications and applications of the gospel, such as the obligation to live justly in the world, though legitimate and important in their own right, are not definitional components of the gospel.

SCRIPTURE: Genesis 3:15; Proverbs 29:18; Isaiah 25:7, 60:2, 3; Romans 1:16–17, 10:14,15,17; 1 Corinthians 15:1–11; Galatians 1:6–9; Revelation 13:8

VII: Salvation

WE AFFIRM that salvation is granted by God's grace alone received through faith alone in Jesus Christ alone. Every believer is united to Christ, justified before God, and adopted into his family. Thus, in God's eyes there is no difference in spiritual value or worth among those who are in Christ. Further, all who are united to Christ are also united to one another regardless of age, ethnicity, or sex. All believers are being conformed to the image

of Christ. By God's regenerating and sanctifying grace all believers will be brought to a final glorified, sinless state of perfection in the day of Jesus Christ.
WE DENY that salvation can be received in any other way. We also deny that salvation renders any Christian free from all remaining sin or immune from even grievous sin in this life. We further deny that ethnicity excludes anyone from understanding the gospel, nor does anyone's ethnic or cultural heritage mitigate or remove the duty to repent and believe.

SCRIPTURE: Genesis 3:15; Acts 20:32; Romans 3–4; Ephesians 2:8–9; Galatians 3:28–29; 1 John 2:1–2

VIII: The Church

WE AFFIRM that the primary role of the church is to worship God through the preaching of his word, teaching sound doctrine, observing baptism and the Lord's Supper, refuting those who contradict, equipping the saints, and evangelizing the lost. We affirm that when the primacy of the gospel is maintained that this often has a positive effect on the culture in which various societal ills are mollified. We affirm that, under the lordship of Christ, we are to obey the governing authorities established by God and pray for civil leaders.

WE DENY that political or social activism should be viewed as integral components of the gospel or primary to the mission of the church. Though believers can and should utilize all lawful means that God has providentially established to have some effect on the laws of a society, we deny that these activities are either evidence of saving faith or constitute a central part of the church's mission given to her by Jesus Christ, her head. We deny that laws or regulations possess any inherent power to change sinful hearts.

SCRIPTURE: Matthew 28:16–20; Romans 13:1–7; 1 Timothy 2:1–3; 2 Timothy 4:2; Titus 1:9; 1 Peter 2:13–17

IX: Heresy

WE AFFIRM that heresy is a denial of or departure from a doctrine that is essential to the Christian faith. We further affirm that heresy often involves the replacement of key, essential truths with variant concepts, or the elevation of non-essentials to the status of essentials. To embrace heresy is to depart from the faith once delivered to the saints and thus to be on a path toward spiritual destruction. We affirm that the accusation of heresy should be reserved for those departures from Christian truth that destroy the weight-bearing doctrines of the redemptive core of Scripture. We affirm that accusations of heresy should be accompanied with clear evidence of such destructive beliefs.

WE DENY that the charge of heresy can be legitimately brought against every failure to achieve perfect conformity to all that is implied in sincere faith in the gospel.

SCRIPTURE: John 14:6; Acts 4:12; Galatians 1:6–9; 1 John 4:1–3, 10, 14, 15; 5:1, 6–12

X: Sexuality and Marriage

WE AFFIRM that God created mankind male and female and that this divinely determined distinction is good, proper, and to be celebrated. Maleness and femaleness are biologically determined at conception and are not subject to change. The curse of sin results in sinful, disordered affections that manifest in some people as same-sex attraction. Salvation grants sanctifying power to renounce such dishonorable affections as sinful and to mortify them by the Spirit. We further affirm that God's design for marriage is that one woman and one man live in a one-flesh, covenantal, sexual relationship until separated by death. Those who lack the desire or opportunity for marriage are called to serve God in singleness and chastity. This is as noble a calling as marriage. WE DENY that human sexuality is a socially constructed concept. We also deny that one's sex can be fluid. We reject "gay Christian" as a legitimate biblical category. We further deny that any kind of partnership or union can properly be called marriage other than one man and one woman in lifelong covenant together. We further deny that people should be identified as "sexual minorities"—which serves as a cultural classification rather than one that honors the image-bearing character of human sexuality as created by God.

SCRIPTURE: Genesis 1:26–27, 2:24, 4:1, 19:24–28; Matthew 19:3–6; Romans 8:13; 1 Corinthians 6:9–11; 1 Timothy 1:10; Jude 7

XI: Complementarianism

WE AFFIRM that God created mankind both male and female with inherent biological and personal distinctions between them and that these created differences are good, proper, and beautiful. Though there is no difference between men and women before God's law or as recipients of his saving grace, we affirm that God has designed men and women with distinct traits and to fulfill distinct roles. These differences are most clearly defined in marriage and the church, but are not irrelevant in other spheres of life. In marriage the husband is to lead, love, and safeguard his wife and the wife is to respect and be submissive to her husband in all things lawful. In the church, qualified men alone are to lead as pastors/elders/bishops and preach to and teach the whole congregation. We further affirm that the image of God is expressed most fully and beautifully in human society when men and women walk in obedience to their God-ordained roles and serve according to their God-given gifts.

WE DENY that the God-ordained differences in men's and women's roles disparage the inherent spiritual worth or value of one over the other, nor do those differences in any way inhibit either men or women from flourishing for the glory of God.

SCRIPTURE: Genesis 1:26–28, 2:15–25, 3:1–24; Ephesians 5:22–33; 1 Corinthians 11:7–9; 1 Timothy 2:12–14; Titus 2

XII: Race / Ethnicity

WE AFFIRM God made all people from one man. Though people often can be distinguished by different ethnicities and nationalities, they are ontological equals before God in both creation and redemption. "Race" is not a biblical category, but rather a social construct that often has been used to classify groups of people in terms of inferiority and superiority. All that is good, honest, just, and beautiful in various ethnic backgrounds and experiences can be celebrated as the fruit of God's grace. All sinful actions and their results (including evils perpetrated between and upon ethnic groups by others) are to be confessed as sinful, repented of, and repudiated.

WE DENY that Christians should segregate themselves into racial groups or regard racial identity above, or even equal to, their identity in Christ. We deny that any divisions between people groups (from an unstated attitude of superiority to an overt spirit of resentment) have any legitimate place in the fellowship of the redeemed. We reject any teaching that encourages racial groups to view themselves as privileged oppressors or entitled victims of oppression. While we are to weep with those who weep, we deny that a person's feelings of offense or oppression necessarily prove that someone else is guilty of sinful behaviors, oppression, or prejudice.

SCRIPTURE: Genesis 1:26–28; Acts 17:24–26; 1 Corinthians 13:4–7; 2 Corinthians 12:16–18

XIII: Culture

WE AFFIRM that some cultures operate on assumptions that are inherently better than those of other cultures because of the biblical truths that inform those worldviews that have produced these distinct assumptions. Those elements of a given culture that reflect divine revelation should be celebrated and promoted. But the various cultures out of which we have been called all have features that are worldly and sinful—and therefore those sinful features should be repudiated for the honor of Christ. We affirm that whatever evil influences to which we have been subjected via our culture can be—and must be—overcome through conversion and the training of both mind and heart through biblical truth.

WE DENY that individuals and sub-groups in any culture are unable, by God's grace, to rise above whatever moral defects or spiritual deficiencies have been engendered or encouraged by their respective cultures.

SCRIPTURE: Romans 1:18–32; Ephesians 4:17–24; Colossians 3:5–11

XIV: Racism

WE AFFIRM that racism is a sin rooted in pride and malice which must be condemned and renounced by all who would honor the image of God in all people. Such racial sin can subtly or overtly manifest itself as racial animosity or racial vainglory. Such sinful prejudice or partiality falls short of God's revealed will and violates the royal law of love. We affirm that virtually all cultures, including our own, at times contain laws and systems that foster racist attitudes and policies.

WE DENY that treating people with sinful partiality or prejudice is consistent with biblical Christianity. We deny that only those in positions of power are capable of racism, or that individuals of any particular ethnic groups are incapable of racism. We deny that systemic racism is in any way compatible with the core principles of historic evangelical convictions. We deny that the Bible can be legitimately used to foster or justify partiality, prejudice, or contempt toward other ethnicities. We deny that the contemporary evangelical movement has any deliberate agenda to elevate one ethnic group and subjugate another. And we emphatically deny that lectures on social issues (or activism aimed at reshaping the wider culture) are as vital to the life and health of the church as the preaching of the gospel and the exposition of Scripture. Historically, such things tend to become distractions that inevitably lead to departures from the gospel.

SCRIPTURE: Genesis 1:26–27; Deuteronomy 10:17; Acts 10:34; Romans 2:11; Ephesians 6:9; Galatians 3:28; James 2:4

3

....

The Christian's Authority

God's Will and the Sexual Revolution

For this is the will of God, your sanctification; that is, that you abstain from sexual immorality; that each of you know how to possess his own vessel in sanctification and honor, not in lustful passion, like the Gentiles who do not know God.

1 Thessalonians 4:3–5

On the eve of His crucifixion, Jesus prayed to His Father: "Sanctify them in the truth; Your word is truth" (John 17:17). In other words, "Father, set them apart for Your purposes alone to do Your will, to think Your thoughts, and to enjoy Your blessing, which can only be accomplished when they live in conformity with Your revealed Word." Jesus knew obedience to the truth of God's Word would bring blessing, and disobedience would bring judgment. And we are experiencing the latter in America today, consistent with the apostle's sorrowful assessment—the inspired Word of God—"Professing to be wise, they became fools . . . . Therefore God gave them over in the lusts of their hearts to impurity, so that their bodies would be dishonored among them. For they exchanged the truth of God for a lie, and worshiped and served the creature rather than the Creator, who is blessed forever. Amen." (Rom. 1:22–24).

There is no greater proof of people's innate hostility towards God's sanctifying truth than the staggering immorality of our postmodern, post-Christian culture—one that utterly rejects the authority of Scripture. This is especially true in matters to do with sexuality, morality, and marriage. Despite just how clear God's righteous standards are as revealed in His Word, the church in America (along with much of evangelicalism worldwide) has caved in to pressure from the ungodly mob of the sexual, homosexual, and transgender revolution. And there is perhaps no issue in America that garners more hatred toward biblical Christianity than this.

Although the average American is horribly offended by what God has to say on this subject and will despise me for explaining it from His Word—the Christian's authority—I do so not out of hateful bigotry, but out of a heart of love for those who are deceived and damned—perhaps eternally so. And I write this for the glory of God whom I love and serve.

Woodstock Lives On

The moral free fall in our culture that began most visibly at the Woodstock music festival in 1969 has gained such momentum that there is more than sufficient evidence to say that America is now experiencing the wrath of divine abandonment in which God has lifted His restraining grace and now allows those who reject Him to experience the hideous consequences of their rebellion: "And just as they did not see fit to acknowledge God any longer, God gave them over to a depraved mind, to do those things which are not proper" (Rom. 1:28).

Moreover, it is appalling to witness the creative yet blasphemous ways the Bible is distorted among many professing Christians in their effort to embrace everything from homosexuality to transgenderism—as if such things are morally acceptable in God's eyes. Worse yet, such blatantly unbiblical positions are boldly touted as being examples of Christian love when just the opposite is true. When the eternal souls of men and women are at stake, there can be no greater act of hatred than to make people comfortable in their sin and thus doom them to God's righteous judgment—like the false prophets who "[strengthened] the hands of evildoers, so that no one has turned back from his wickedness. All of them have become to Me like Sodom, and her inhabitants like Gomorrah. . . . They are leading you into futility; they speak a vision of their own imagination, not from the mouth of the LORD" (Jer. 23:14, 16).

I have seen firsthand the dramatic conversion of people who were enslaved to many different forms of sexual perversions, and I marvel at the radically transforming power of the gospel. Every Christian can rejoice in the words of the apostle Paul who, after warning fornicators, idolaters, adulterers, homosexuals, and sodomites that they would not enter the kingdom of God unless they embraced Christ in repentant faith (1 Cor. 6:9), went on to add these encouraging words: "Such were some of you; but you were washed, but you were sanctified, but you were justified in the name of the Lord Jesus Christ and in the Spirit of our God" (1 Cor. 6:11).

People who ignore God's standards of righteousness take for granted His merciful patience, even though this is meant to lead them to repentance and forgiveness. As a result, they foolishly think that His delay in sending punishment means He is indifferent, tolerant, or perhaps even in agreement. What they fail to realize is that God's compassionate delay in judgment also provides a season in which rebellious sinners can further harden their heart against the truths they are resisting—and so they accumulate a greater store of wrath. This is a very dangerous reality that is too often ignored. Paul described it this way:

> Or do you think lightly of the riches of His kindness and tolerance and patience, not knowing that the kindness of God leads you to repentance? But because of your stubbornness and unrepentant heart you are storing up wrath for yourself in the day of wrath and revelation of the righteous judgment of God, who will render to each person according to his deeds.
> (Rom. 2:4–6)

God's Judgment on Sodom and Gomorrah

The forbidden perversion of homosexuality (Lev. 18:22, 29; 20:13; Rom. 1:26; 1 Cor. 6:9; 1 Tim. 1:10) ignited God's judgment upon ancient Sodom and Gomorrah and the surrounding cities (Gen. 14:8; *cf.* Jude 7), when "the LORD rained on Sodom and Gomorrah brimstone and fire from the LORD out of heaven" (Gen. 19:24). Even Lot was "oppressed by the sensual conduct of unprincipled men" in Sodom, "for by what he saw and heard that righteous man, while living among them, felt his righteous soul tormented day after day by their lawless deeds" (2 Peter 2:7, 8). The heart of every Christian should likewise feel tormented by the rampant immorality that now defines our culture and is now being promoted in apostate churches that are Christian in name only.

But if we, in our humanity, are relatively unholy (and yet so grievously offended and distressed), what must be the reaction of God who is most holy? The answer is in Romans 1:19: "For the wrath of God is revealed from heaven against all ungodliness and unrighteousness of men who suppress the truth in unrighteousness." Peter described the judgment of God that reduced Sodom and Gomorrah to ashes because of their citizens' sexual deviancy as "an example to those who would live ungodly lives thereafter" (2 Peter 2:6). Jude also cited those two cities as examples of the kinds of sexual immorality and perversions of which the impostors he was confronting were accused, writing,

> Just as Sodom and Gomorrah and the cities around them,
> since they in the same way as these indulged in gross im-
> morality and went after strange flesh, are exhibited as an
> example in undergoing the punishment of eternal fire.
> (Jude 7)

The Sexual Immorality of Ancient Corinth

The Greco-Roman world of the first century had no moral com-
pass. The city of Corinth is a great example. Its people were exceedingly immoral. The most prominent edifice on the acropolis
in Corinth was the Temple to Aphrodite, the Greek goddess of
beauty, love, and procreation, where all manner of ritual prostitution and other vile forms of religious degeneracy were part of
their "worship." Their debauchery was so pervasive and so vile
that even the pagans blushed at it, so much so that they adopted the phrase, "to corinthianize" ("to behave like a Corinthian")
to express the grossest kinds of sexual immorality and drunken
decadence.

Temple excavations in Corinth have discovered thousands
of terracotta votive offerings presented to Asklepios, the god
of healing, and his daughter, Hygieia. Worshippers who sought
healing would come to the temple to sleep and allow non-
poisonous snakes to slither over them. The symbol of Asklepios
was the snake. In fact, our modern medical emblem of a serpent
entwined around a staff comes partially from this ancient cult.
However, this demonic mythology can be traced back to ancient
Egyptian, Sumerian, and Babylonian cultism where similar
symbols were used. It should not escape our notice that Satan is
often symbolized as a crafty serpent, even as he appeared to Eve
in the Garden.

The Lord later describes him in Revelation 12:9 as "the serpent
of old who is called the devil and Satan, who deceives the whole
world." Ancient Gnosticism also used the emblem of a serpent as
the embodiment of the wisdom transmitted by Sophia.

Clay molds of various body parts, including various limbs,

fingers, hands, feet, lips, noses, ears, breasts, male and female genitals, etc., were found in some of the chambers of these ancient Corinthian temples. Clay copies of human body parts were hung around the temple by worshippers in need of healing. But sadly, they did not know their diseased body parts were the result of the dreadful sexually transmitted disease of syphilis—a bacterial infection that can lie dormant for weeks, even decades, before becoming active again. Left untreated, this disease is fatal.

Even as God created and sustains a *physical order* to the universe that operates on fixed, inviolable laws of physics (like the law of gravity), He has also decreed a *moral order* to the universe. Though the consequences of violating His moral order are not always *immediate*, they are *inevitable* because God is holy and just, and therefore all sin must be punished (Rom. 1:18). That grisly scene of hanging body parts paints a graphic picture of sin and people's enslavement to it, for indeed, "There is a way that seems right to a man, but it is the way of death" (Prov. 14:12). People disobey God thinking there's no consequence to their actions, yet all the while the wicked rebellion of their heart is metastasizing, corrupting both body and soul.

We see the physical consequences in diseases like HIV/AIDS and other forms of sexually transmitted diseases. A new strain of gonorrhea ("super gonorrhea") has now surfaced—a venereal disease that is reported to be resistant to all antibiotics normally used to treat the disease. This is truly terrifying since, according to the World Health Organization, gonorrhea infects approximately 87 million men and women every year.[22] It can even spread perinatally from mother to baby during childbirth.

Like idolaters today, the ancient pagans refused to worship the one true God. "Therefore God gave them over in the lusts of their hearts to impurity, that their bodies might be dishonored among them" (Rom. 1:24). No doubt that macabre scene of hanging body parts in the pagan temples influenced Paul's imagery of our bodies being a temple of the Holy Spirit (1 Cor. 6:19) and individual members of the body of Christ (1 Cor. 12:27).

---

22 https://www.who.int/news-room/fact-sheets/detail/sexually-transmitted-infections-(stis)

The Sexual Revolution and Its Consequences

The apostle Paul's words recorded in the inspired text of Romans 1:24–32 are the most sobering and terrifying section in his epistle. They should cause each of us to shiver with solemn reflection about ourselves, and those we know and love. Here we learn what happens *when God rejects man because man has rejected God*. Here we see the tragic consequences when God removes all restraint and lets a society indulge its every lust. When a culture reaches this stage of depravity, God allows it to gradually experience the terrible miseries of its sinful choices. This is best described as the *wrath of divine abandonment*—a terrifying fate that can lead to eternal abandonment for those who never repent.

To express this, three times Paul uses the phrase, "God gave them over" (vv. 24, 26, 28). This translates the Greek verb *paradidōmi*, a very strong word meaning to "deliver up" used in the New Testament in a judicial sense to refer to one who is handed over to another for judgment (Matt. 5:25; 10:17, 19, 21; 18:34). In this context, God "delivers up" or "gives a man over" to the folly of his sin, causing him to experience the miserable consequences it will bring. Why? That he might finally come to a place of repentance, thus making God's abandonment a final act of mercy.

Here we discover three progressive stages of this abandonment—stages not necessarily found in every individual but in the collective whole of a culture that magnifies its rebellion against God primarily through gross immorality. Each stage becomes progressively worse in its evil and in its consequences. First, God gives them over to *sordid immorality*, second, to *shameless homosexuality*, and finally, to *shocking depravity*.

Stage One:
Sordid Immorality—a Violation of God's Moral Order

Paul describes this first stage of divine abandonment by saying, "Therefore God gave them over in the lusts of their hearts to impurity, that their bodies might be dishonored among them" (Rom. 1:24). This speaks of a *perversion of God's moral order that limits*

*sexual activity to the union of one man and one woman in the God-or-
dained covenant of marriage* (Gen. 2:23–24; *cf.* Matt. 19:4–6; Eph.
5:31–32). Paul underscores this principle when he says, "But because of the temptation to sexual immorality, each man should
have his own wife and each woman her own husband" (1 Cor. 7:2).

The Greek term *epithumeō* (translated "lust") simply denotes
the idea of longing or desiring a specific object. In biblical terms,
a desire can be good or bad, depending upon the object desired.
It is translated *lust* when the object desired is bad, and *desire* if
the object has a neutral connotation (e.g., 1 Tim. 3:1). Here in
Romans 1:24, Paul uses the term "lust" (*epithumeō*) to describe evil
cravings, immoral desires, and yearnings for what God forbids.

Jesus uses the same term in Matthew 5:28 when He says, "You
have heard that it was said, 'You shall not commit adultery'; but
I say to you that everyone who looks at a woman with *lust* for her
has already committed adultery with her in his heart" (emphasis
mine). Lusting after a woman (or a man) proves a person "has
already committed adultery" in his or her heart. Said differently,
lust is a manifestation of an immoral heart rooted in our sinful
nature. James warns: "Each one is tempted when he is carried
away and enticed by his own lust" (James 1:14). Whenever the
object of one's desire is for what God forbids, the desire itself is
sinful. Paul categorizes it as "the desire of the flesh . . . . For the
flesh sets its desire against the Spirit" (Gal. 5:15). This also refutes
the unbiblical notion that *same-sex attraction*—often referred to
as *homosexual orientation*—is morally neutral unless it is acted
upon since, as some will argue, "a person cannot help how God
created them." What they fail to understand is the attraction itself
is sinful.

Jesus makes it clear that lust is rooted in "their hearts" (*kardia*),
referring to the governing faculty of the person (Matt. 18:35;
Rom. 6:17; 2 Cor. 5:12). The heart is the locus of man's thoughts,
conscience, will, and emotion—that inner core and basic nature
of who he really is as a person. It is the heart that "is more deceitful
than all else and is desperately sick" (Jer. 17:9; *cf.* Prov. 4:23). For
this reason Solomon said, "The hearts of the sons of men are full
of evil, and insanity is in their hearts throughout their lives" (Eccl.
9:3). Jesus described it this way: "For out of the heart come evil

thoughts, murders, adulteries, fornications, thefts, false witness, slanders. These are the things which defile the man" (Matt. 15:19–20). Paul reminded the believers in Ephesus about this very thing, saying, "We too all formerly lived in the lusts of our flesh, indulging the desires of the flesh and of the mind, and were by nature children of wrath, even as the rest" (Eph. 2:3).

Craving Impurity and Moral Degradation

So what we see thus far in this first stage of divine abandonment is that people who reject God are given over to their lusts because they have a heart craving for "impurity" (*akatharsia*), meaning "uncleanness" or "filth." This was a term used to describe the putrefaction of a corpse or the contents of a grave, which also became a synonym for sexual immorality. Paul used it in 2 Corinthians 12:21 where he expressed his concern for those "who had sinned in the past and not repented of the *impurity*, immorality and sensuality which they [had] practiced" (emphasis mine). The unregenerate are described as those who "walk, in the futility of their mind, being darkened in their understanding, excluded from the life of God because of the ignorance that is in them, because of the hardness of their heart; and they, having become callous, *have given themselves over to sensuality for the practice of every kind of impurity with greediness*" (Eph. 4:17b–19; emphasis mine).

Here we learn that when a man persistently rejects God, God will gradually give him over to a carnal craving for forbidden kinds of sexual immorality, as we see in American culture. Then notice the consequence: ". . . that their bodies might be dishonored among them." (Rom. 1:24b). When people indulge in these kinds of sins, their bodies are "dishonored" (*atimazō*), which means they are *treated shamefully and characterized by dishonor and a lack of respect.* The immediate context would indicate that Paul had fertility cult ritual prostitution and habitual sexual contact with them in mind—central to their idolatrous practices. But their immoral worship would have also fueled the innate prurience of their depraved heart, spawning gross immorality at every level of their society as well.

Prowling Dogs and Alley Cats

Our American culture can be likened to prowling dogs and alley cats, utterly bereft of moral principles and dignity. Our women—including young girls—dress like trollops showing as much skin as possible (the tighter the clothing, the better), and our men mentally undress them as they walk by. Nothing causes us to blush anymore. The dirtier, the better; and no one seems to care—not even in many churches. Hosea's warning is fitting for many within the ranks of evangelicalism today when he said, "Their deeds will not allow them to return to their God. For a spirit of harlotry is within them, and they do not know the LORD" (Hosea 5:4).

Given this, we should not be dismayed at the irrationality of our political leaders, the riots in our streets, and the rapid demise of common decency and decorum in our culture. There is nothing sacred anymore, not even the sanctity of marriage between a man and a woman. Our country has become a nation of idolatrous sex worshippers and is now experiencing the wrath of divine abandonment! When a nation exchanges the truth of God for a lie, it will be *delivered over to that lie to become its slave and ultimately be destroyed by it*. God will abandon it to *sordid immorality—a violation of God's moral order* that will give rise to stage two: *shameless homosexuality—an inversion of God's created order.*

Stage Two:
Shameless Homosexuality—
An Inversion of God's Created Order

The next stage in the progression is described in Romans 1:26: "For this reason God gave them over to degrading passions, for their women [lit. females] exchanged the natural function for that which is unnatural." The term "degrading" (*atimia*) speaks of that which is vile, disgraceful, or shameful. God abandons them to the vile affections of homosexuality.

Once again, in context, this is what happens when individuals exchange the truth of who God is for a lie. *Righteousness* will then be exchanged for that which is *unrighteous*, and what is *pure* will be exchanged for what is *unclean*. Paul's use of "the natural" (*phusikos*) refers to that which is produced by nature, inborn, governed by the instincts of nature, and the term "function" (*chresis*) simply means "use"—the sexual use of a woman, referring to the normal, natural intimacy of sexual intercourse. That is exchanged "for that which is unnatural" (against nature, contrary to instincts that govern our behavior).

Obviously this is speaking of homosexual behavior among women. Unlike "sordid immorality" (a perversion of God's intention for sexual relations), homosexuality is an inversion of not only God's intentions for sexual relations, but it also defies man's nature that instinctively governs his behaviors. It is interesting that Paul mentions female homosexuality first, and male homosexuality second. Since females in a society are generally more reluctant than men to fall prey to sordid immorality—especially shameless homosexuality—perhaps by mentioning them first Paul is describing a culture where this form of idolatry is so rampant that all moral virtue has disappeared. That is certainly true in our Western culture.

The Inner Inferno of Homosexual Lust

He then goes on to add, "and in the same way also the men abandoned the natural function of the woman and burned in their desire toward one another, men with men committing indecent acts . . ." (Rom. 1:27). The term "burned" (*ekkaio*) means "to set on fire" or "to inflame." Because it is in the passive voice, he's saying, "They are set on fire in their desire." They become inflamed or consumed with an unnatural craving to be sexually involved with another man. It is not at all uncommon for homosexual men to have over 110 partners per year, although females average only one or two.

For those not enslaved by this sin, it is impossible to conceive of anything so life dominating. Genesis 19 provides an example of this in the account of the two angels that came to visit Lot in the city of Sodom. On seeing the strangers "the men of the city, the men of Sodom, surrounded the house, both young and old, all the people from every quarter; and they called to Lot and said to him,

"Where are the men who came to you tonight? Bring them out to us that we may have relations with them. . . ." They pressed hard against Lot and came near to break the door. But the men reached out their hands and brought Lot into the house with them, and shut the door. And they struck the men who were at the doorway of the house with blindness, both small and great, so that they wearied themselves trying to find the doorway.
(Gen. 19:5, 9–11)

Amazing! Their lust was so strong that despite being supernaturally blinded, they still exhausted themselves to find the doorway to break in and have their way with the strangers. The text goes on to say that this sin was so great in Sodom and Gomorrah that God rained down fire and brimstone out of heaven upon them and utterly destroyed them. Unlike any other place in the world, deposits of sulfur (brimstone) capsules with a purity of 98 percent can still be found in layers of ash in this region. From Genesis 19 onward, the word "sodomy" is used to describe homosexuality.

Paul went on to describe this perversion in Romans 1:27 saying, "Men abandoned the natural function of the woman and burned in their desire toward one another, men with men committing indecent acts" (*aschemosune*: "that which is unseemly" or "shameful"; "males with males perpetrating shamelessness" [KJV]). How sad that they want to be called "gay" when they are anything but gay; they are filled with shame, guilt, frustration, helplessness, hopelessness, and rage. Yet they are constantly promoting "gay pride." This is reminiscent of the homosexual rebellion that contributed to the societal collapse of ancient Judah and triggered God's judgment upon them:

For Jerusalem has stumbled and Judah has fallen, because their speech and their actions are against the LORD, to rebel against His glorious presence. The expression of their faces bears witness against them, and they display their sin like Sodom; they do not even conceal it. Woe to them! For they have brought evil on themselves.
(Isa. 3:8–9)

Unfortunately, most Americans reject, ignore, or deliberately distort God's Word on this matter, despite how clearly He has spoken on the subject (e.g., Lev. 18:22; 20:13; Deut. 23:17; Judg. 19:22–24; 1 Kings 14:24; 1 Cor. 6:9; Eph. 4:17; 1 Tim. 1:9). Nevertheless, it is the responsibility of believers—especially ministers of the gospel—to make this clear, praying that the seeds of truth will fall on fertile hearts and produce the fruits of righteousness and blessing.

Chilling Examples of Homosexual Conduct and Consequences

Having counseled homosexual men, and having worked closely with doctors and nurses who have attended them in the emergency rooms in local hospitals, I know far more than I wish I knew about the bizarre sexual practices in that community—sexual activities so vile that they can only be described as demonic. And sadly, but not surprisingly, their unsanitary activities in disease-ridden places not only transmit bacteria, parasites, and facilitate the spread of hepatitis B, HIV, syphilis, and numerous other blood-borne diseases, but they also tear rectal tissues.[23] But none of this should surprise us. Even Josephus, *Antiquities.* 1.194, stated that they "abused themselves with Sodomitical practices."[24]

Even as God has determined fixed, inviolable *laws of physics* to maintain the order of His physical order, so too He has determined fixed, inviolable *laws of morality* to maintain His moral order. The self-avenging nature of sexual perversion is evidence of what happens when a person violates God's law of morality, as in this case, "men with men committing indecent [shameful] acts and receiving in their own persons the due penalty of their error" (Rom. 1:27). Can there be a more tragic example of this than AIDS?

In their excellent book, *Transforming Homosexuality: What the Bible Says About Sexual Orientation and Change,* Denny Burk and Heath Lambert offer additional insight into the many physical ways in which, under the moral management of God, gross immorality triggers its own "due penalty" (Rom. 1:27):

---

23 http://www.familyresearchinst.org/2009/02/medical-consequences-of-what-homosexuals-do/
24 P. H. Davids, *The Letters of 2 Peter and Jude* (Grand Rapids, Michigan: William B. Eerdmans Pub. Co., 2006), 53.

Homosexuality is dangerous. *The Journal of the American Medical Association* reports that male homosexuals experience a 4,000 percent higher risk of anal cancer than the rest of the population. Male homosexuals with a long-term partner live, on average, thirty years shorter than heterosexual men. These and other factors are why homosexual men are at such high risk for emotional and spiritual problems.[25]

They went on to say that "This was the conclusion of J. Michael Bailey concerning several studies on homosexuality:

These studies contain arguably the best published data on the association between homosexuality and psychopathology, and both converge on the same unhappy conclusion: homosexual people are at substantially higher risk for some forms of emotional problems, including suicidality, major depression, and anxiety disorder, [and] conduct disorder.[26]

According to the Family Research Institute:

The median age of death for homosexuals . . . was virtually the same nationwide—and, overall, about 2% survived to old age. If AIDS was the listed cause of death, the median age was 39. For the 829 gays who were listed as dying of something other than AIDS, the median age of death was 42 and 9% died old. The 163 lesbians had a median age of death of 44 and 20% died old.

Even when AIDS was apparently not involved, homosexuals frequently met an early demise. Three percent of gays died violently. They were 116 times more apt to be murdered (compared to national murder rates), much more apt to commit suicide, and had high traffic-accident death-rates. Heart attacks, cancer, and liver failure were exceptionally common. 18% of lesbians died of murder, suicide, or accidents—a rate 456 times higher than that of white females

25   Denny Burk and Heath Lambert, *Transforming Homosexuality: What the Bible Says About Sexual Orientation and Change* (Phillipsburg, New Jersey: P&R Publishing, 2015), 72.
26   J. M. Bailey, "Homosexuality and Mental Illness," *Archives of General Psychiatry* 56, no. 10 (October 1999), 883–84.

aged 25–44. Age distributions of samples of homosexuals in the scientific literature from 1858 to 1997 suggest a similarly shortened lifespan.

Follow-up studies of homosexual longevity have confirmed these general results. Comparison of gay obituaries who died of AIDS to official U.S. HIV/AIDS Surveillance data demonstrated very close agreement between the estimated median ages of death, as well as the 25th and 75th percentiles of the age-at-death distribution. Another study looked at multiple lines of evidence—including more recent U.S. obituaries and patterns of homosexual partnerships in Scandinavia—again finding that homosexual behavior was associated with a shortening of life of probably two decades.[27]

It is obvious to any unbiased observer that the inevitable temporal penalty of homosexuality is the consequences of the perversion itself—"men with men committing indecent acts and receiving in their own persons the due penalty of their error" (Rom. 1:27). However, unless they come to Christ in repentant faith and experience the transforming power of regeneration, the eternal consequences will be infinitely worse: "Just as Sodom and Gomorrah and the cities around them . . . indulged in gross immorality and went after strange flesh, are . . . undergoing the punishment of eternal fire" (Jude 7; *cf.* Rev. 21:8).

Once again, when man rejects God, God rejects man, and gives him over to *sordid immorality, shameless homosexuality,* which leads to the final stage of *shocking depravity.*

Stage Three:
Shocking Depravity—
A Disposition of Godless Corruption

The correlation in Romans 1:24 and 26 between man's arrogant rejection of God and God's righteous rejection of man is stated again in verse 28: "And just as they did not see fit to acknowledge God any longer, God gave them over to a depraved mind, to do

---

27 http://www.familyresearchinst.org/2009/02/medical-consequences-of-what-homosexuals-do/

those things which are not proper." The "depraved mind" shakes its fist in God's face and says, "Depart from us! We do not even desire the knowledge of Your ways. Who is the Almighty, that we should serve Him, and what would we gain if we entreat Him?" (Job 21:14–15).

Paul's use of the term "depraved" is most telling; it explains the utter irrationality and insanity that is now so pervasive in American culture. The Greek term *adokimos*, translated "depraved," means "unapproved," "worthless," "useless." It was originally used to describe worthless metals rejected by refiners due to their impurity. In context, the phrase highlights a frightening reality: when man ignores all the evidence of nature and conscience and refuses to "approve" of God, he will be given over to an "unapproved" mind that is utterly worthless—*a disposition of godless corruption*. This is similarly stated in Titus 1:15–16: "To those who are defiled and unbelieving, nothing is pure, but both their mind and their conscience are defiled. They profess to know God, but by their deeds they deny Him, being detestable and disobedient and worthless for any good deed." Our culture's obsession with transgenderism is a prime example of a depraved mind.

Rather than rejoicing in God's goodness in creating a child in His image as male and female, an increasing number of parents embrace "Gender-Creative" parenting where children are allowed to discover their own gender identity. According to Healthline. com there are now sixty-four terms that describe gender identity and expression.[28] And what is even more shocking is the culture's acceptance of this kind of insanity. Dr. Michael A. Milton writes:

> Humankind's potential for self-destruction through the lusts of the flesh appears to be limitless. While there is nothing new in the sensual sins and wanton debauchery that we witness in our culture, technology has undoubtedly advanced its influence. And one such sin is being promoted in an apparently fanatical fashion: *transgenderism*.
>
> The subject of transgenderism, includes, specifically, *"Trans-sexuality, cross-dressing,"* and seeking *"gender identity*

---

28   https://www.healthline.com/health/different-genders

development," i.e., physical identity through radical surgeries, and hormone treatment; and, more broadly, "gender atypicality" that includes "myriad subcultural expressions of self-selecting gender," and "intersectionality" with other "interdependence" movements, i.e., feminism, homosexuality. The idea of transgenderism has its roots in the primordial rebellion of humankind to the creation order of God.

Ancient pagan rituals would have included some aspects of transgender practice. More currently, social anarchists such as the otherwise brilliant French social critic, Michael Foucault, argued that Christianity, in particular, has leveraged its cultural "powers" (a recurring theme with Foucault) to repress human sexual expression. Foucault taught that gender is a social construct, not a biological fact. The absurdity of such thinking was largely unchallenged in the 1960s and 70s when Foucault and others were teach such dogma in prestigious universities in Canada, France, and the United States.

Recently, in 2019, when a former United States Vice-President was asked how many genders there were, he responded, "At least three." Such a frighteningly fallacious response by a person of influence constitutes an unmitigated endorsement of Foucault's radical deconstruction of reality. For someone to affirm, with a straight face, in serious dialogues, "There are at least three genders" is an Orwellian case study in "doublethink," "newspeak," and the "thought police" writ large. To speak seriously about a gender other than male and female is surely the untenable subordinating to the inconceivable.[29]

But the shocking depravity of "a depraved mind, to do those things which are not proper" includes a vast array of vices beyond the illustration of transgenderism. Paul goes on to give a representative sample in Romans 1:29–31 describing the wickedness that characterizes a people given to idolatry and the concomitant immorality associated with it. He describes them as "being filled with" (v. 29), meaning they are wholly given over to the following:

29 https://www.biblestudytools.com/bible-study/topical-studies/what-the-bible-really-says-about-transgenderism.html

- "all unrighteousness" (*adikia*): those whose heart and life-style consistently violate God's moral standard of righteousness found in His law (*cf.* Rom. 3:10–18).
- "wickedness" (*ponēria*): a synonym for unrighteousness describing those who enjoy perverting virtue and moral principles to do evil (*cf.* Jer. 4:22: 1 Cor. 6:9–10; Gal. 5:19–21; Col. 3:5).
- "greed" (*pleonexia*): those with an insatiable appetite for more and more possessions, never content or satisfied, bent on gaining what they desire no matter how it is achieved (*cf.* Mark 7:22; Eph. 6:12).
- "evil" (*kakia*): those filled with malice, cruelty, and a desire to injure others, unashamed to break the law (*cf.* Gen. 6:5; Isa. 5:20; 13:11; Gal. 1:4).
- "full of envy" (*phthonos*): those who are aroused to anger toward the success or possessions of another and begrudge them for having it (*cf.* Titus 3:3; James 3:16).
- "murder" (*phonos*): the unlawful killing of one human being by another. All the previous vices lead to this, especially envy (*cf.* Ex. 20:13; 1 Tim. 1:9).
- "strife" (*eris*): those who are habitually involved in bitter conflict, contentious debate, violent dissension (*cf.* Prov. 10:12; 13:10; 16:28; James 4:1).
- "deceit" (*dolos*): those who are cunningly dishonest, skilled in treachery, disingenuous, duplicitous, and crafty in lying (*cf.* Jer. 17:9; Rom. 3:13; 2 Tim. 3:13).
- "malice" (*kakoētheia*): those with a spiteful, cruel, depraved character, who are malicious and wily in harming other people (*cf.* 1 Cor. 5:8; Eph. 4:31; Titus 3:3).
- "they are gossips" (*psithyristēs*): those who whisper, a secret slanderer who vilifies others and spreads rumors to harm them (*cf.* Prov. 16:28; 2 Cor. 12:20).
- "slanderers" (*katalalos*): those who speak evil of others in order to destroy their reputation (*cf.* Ex. 20:16; Lev. 19:16; Prov. 6:19).
- "haters of God" (*theostygēs*): those with excessive contempt for God (*cf.* Num. 10:35; Deut. 7:10; Rom. 8:7–8; James 4:4).
- "insolent" (*hubristēs*): those who are brazenly insulting, out-

rageously disrespectful and offensive, a "violent aggressor" (*cf.* 1 Tim 1:13).

- "arrogant" (*hyperēphanos*): those who are characterized by feelings of unwarranted importance, who consider themselves superior to others and despise those considered beneath them, treating them with contempt (*cf.* Ps. 94:3–7; Prov. 8:13; Isa. 13:11).
- "boastful" (*alazōn*): those who are a self-absorbed, a self-exalting braggart; an empty pretender proud without cause; one who is a legend in his or her own mind (*cf.* Isa. 14:13–16; Ps. 10:3; Prov. 25:14).
- "inventors of evil" (*epheuretēs kakos*): those who delight in devising novel forms of evil to destroy others and derive pleasure in finding new and creative ways to mock God (*cf.* Ps. 106:34–39; Prov. 24:8–9; Eccl. 7:29).
- "disobedient to parents" (*apeithēs goneus*): those who refuse to submit the parental authority God has placed over them (*cf.* Ex. 20:12; 21:15, 17; Prov. 20:20; Matt. 15:4).
- "without understanding" (*asynetos*): those who are senseless, stupid, foolish, undiscerning (*cf.* Prov. 18:2; Jer. 4:22; Rom. 3:11; 1 Cor. 2:14).
- "untrustworthy" (*asynthetos*): covenant breakers, those who disregard contracts and marital vows, and whose word means nothing (*cf.* Ps. 78:57; 119:158; Matt. 5:37).
- "unloving" (*astorgos*): those who are heartless toward those they should love; especially bereft of the natural affection toward children and family members (*cf.* Lev. 18:21; Ps. 106:36–38).
- "unmerciful" (*aneleēmōn*): those who are cruel, ruthless, merciless, heartless, and unsympathetic (*cf.* Matt. 18:32–34; James 2:13).

Examples of these crimes abound in our culture. Indeed, people are "filled with" them (Rom. 1:29). But Paul states the very pinnacle of perversity in verse 32: "and, although they know the ordinance of God, that those who practice such things are worthy of death," since God has revealed it to them in nature (Rom. 1:20) and conscience (Rom. 2:14–15), "they not only do the same, but also give hearty approval to those who practice them." This is *shocking depravity*! Although their conscience is animated by the horrific fear of divine judgment, their heart has been so hardened by the deceitfulness of sin (Heb. 3:13) that they not only continue to "practice these things" but they encourage others to do the same. Indeed, today's society glamorizes the most deviant forms of sexual immorality. It elects officials to legalize, promote, and protect all manner of perversions. It worships artists and actors and authors and comedians who will advance the causes of the wicked and perverse. What should be considered shameful is exalted under rainbow banner of "Pride!"

Defiant Debauchery

This is reminiscent of the defiant debauchery of ancient Judah that inflamed God's wrath against them and unleashed His judgment upon them. Using bitter words in Isaiah 5:18, God spoke through His prophet saying: "Woe to those who drag iniquity with the cords of falsehood, and sin as if with cart ropes; who say, 'Let Him make speed, let Him hasten His work, that we may see it; and let the purpose of the Holy One of Israel draw near and come to pass, that we may know it!'" The imagery is that of beasts of burden dragging the sins of the people around in decorated floats, flaunting their sins publicly, defying God, and daring Him to judge them—which in fact He did—and which He will do to any nation that defies Him.

This is *the wrath of divine abandonment*: "But My people did not listen to My voice, and Israel did not obey Me. So I gave them over to the stubbornness of their heart, to walk in their own devices" (Ps. 81:11-12). And through Hosea, He lamented, "Ephraim is joined to idols; let him alone" (4:17). Sadly, this is the state of the United States of America today.

It has exchanged the truth of God for a lie and has now been delivered over to that lie to become its slave and ultimately be destroyed by it. As a result, God first gave our nation over to *sordid immorality—a violation of His moral order,* then *shameless homosexually—an inversion of his created order,* and now, a people characterized by *shocking depravity—a disposition of godless corruption.* The psalmist summarized our tragic fate this way: "The wicked will return to Sheol, *even* all the nations who forget God" (Ps. 9:17). The only hope for any nation or any individual is repentant faith in the Lord Jesus Christ.

A Promise of
Forgiveness, Deliverance, and Transformation

Scripture is clear, and any honest self-assessment will affirm that we are all sinners. Adam's sin has affected all of us, not only as it relates to the legal guilt that God imputes to us (Rom. 5:18–19), but also with respect to the sinful nature we inherited (Ps. 51:5). Prior to salvation, the disposition of our nature to disobey and displease God was so powerful and pervasive that Paul affirmed, "We were by nature children of wrath, like the rest of mankind" (Eph. 2:3). Nothing about us was pleasing to Him, for "those who are in the flesh cannot please God" (Rom. 8:8). Indeed, "without faith it is impossible to please Him" (Heb. 11:6), because we "were dead in [our] trespasses and sins, in which [we] formerly walked" (Eph. 2:1–2). Wayne Grudem has rightly stated,

> It is not just that some parts of us are sinful and others are pure. Rather, every part of our being is affected by sin— our intellects, our emotions and desires, our goals and motives, and even our physical bodies. Paul says, "I know that nothing good dwells within me, that is, in my flesh" (Rom. 7:18), and, "to the corrupt and unbelieving nothing is pure; their very minds and consciences are corrupted" (Titus 1:15). Moreover, Jeremiah tells us that "the heart is deceitful above all things, and desperately corrupt; who can understand it?" (Jer. 17:9). In these passages Scripture is not denying that unbelievers can do good in human society *in some senses*. But it is denying that they can do any *spiritual* good or be good *in terms of a relationship with God*. Apart from the work of Christ in our lives, we are like all other unbelievers who are "darkened in their understanding, alienated from the life of God because of

the ignorance that is in them, due to their hardness of heart" (Eph. 4:18).[30]

With these reminders of who we were prior to God's saving and transforming grace, every Christian must admit that we bear the same marks of Adam's sin as the most sexually deviant among us. Our attitude toward them must therefore never be one of hostility, but one of loving identity. While we are no longer incarcerated in the dungeon of unredeemed humanness, enslaved by sin, we must honestly admit that in varying ways we were once just like them. For this reason, it would be the height of haughtiness to harbor animosity toward even the most sexually deviant. While we abhor their sin, we love them for the sake of the gospel, ever mindful of our own sin and undeserved mercy. After listing a number of life-dominating sins that would certainly apply to each of us in one way or another, Paul made this humbling statement: *"Such were some of you*; but you were washed, but you were sanctified, but you were justified in the name of the Lord Jesus Christ and in the Spirit of our God"* (1 Cor. 6:11; emphasis mine).

Thankfully, God has provided a way for sinners to not only be forgiven, but also to be justified, sanctified, and glorified. And this is the ineffably glorious promise of the gospel. Please know there is forgiveness, deliverance, and transformation for those enslaved by illicit sexual desires, including the desires associated with same-sex attraction. Burk and Lambert offer this insightful analysis,

Sin is not merely what we do. It is also who we are. As so many of our confessions have it, we are sinners by nature and by choice. All of us are born with an orientation toward sin. The ongoing experience of same-sex sexual attraction is but one manifestation of our common experience of in-dwelling sin—indeed of the mind set on the flesh (Rom. 7:23; 8:7). For that reason, the Bible teaches us to war against both the root and the fruit of sin. In this case, same-sex attraction is the root, and same-sex sexual behavior is the fruit. The Spirit of God aims to transform both (Rom. 8:13). . . . This is

---

30   Wayne Grudem, *Systematic Theology* (Grand Rapids, Michigan: Zondervan Publishing House, 1994), 497.

not to say that Christians who experience same-sex attraction will necessarily be freed from those desires completely in this life. Many such Christians report partial or complete changes in their attractions after conversion—sometimes all at once, but more often over a period of months and years. But those cases are not the norm. There are a great many who also report ongoing struggles with same-sex attraction. But that does not lessen the responsibility for them to fight those desires as long as they persist, no matter how natural those desires may feel. The Bible teaches that the Holy Spirit can bring about this kind of transformation in anyone—even if such a progress is not experienced by everyone in precisely the same measure. As the apostle Paul writes, "Thanks be to God that though you were slaves of sin, you became obedient from the heart to that form of teaching to which you were committed" (Rom. 6:7).[31]

The Miracle of the New Birth

God has promised to not only forgive, but also radically transform the inner man of those who truly come to Him in repentant faith and trust in Christ as their only hope of salvation. This is the miracle of *regeneration (palingenesia)*, which refers to *a supernatural, instantaneous impartation of spiritual life to the spiritually dead characterized by both washing and renewal.* Paul used the term in Titus 3:5–7: "He saved us, not on the basis of deeds which we have done in righteousness, but according to His mercy, by *the washing of regeneration and renewing by the Holy Spirit,* whom He poured out upon us richly through Jesus Christ our Savior, so that being justified by His grace we would be made heirs according to *the* hope of eternal life" (emphasis mine). This is what Jesus referred to in John 3 when He told Nicodemus, the great teacher of Israel, "You must be born again" (v. 7); "Truly, Truly, I say to you, unless one is born again he cannot see the kingdom of God" (v. 3); and again in verse 5 Jesus said, "Truly, truly, I say to you, unless one is born of water and the Spirit he cannot enter into the kingdom of God."

---

31 Denny Burk and Heath Lambert, *Transforming Homosexuality: What the Bible Says About Sexual Orientation and Change* (Phillipsburg, New Jersey: P&R Publishing, 2015), 58–59.

Regeneration is the Spirit-wrought transformation in the soul that causes an individual to see the dreadful condition of his or her sinful heart, and the undeserved mercy, grace, and love of Christ that he or she now embraces in saving faith. Every true believer can identify with this, in contrast with the unregenerate who are often "Christian" in name only and therefore remain enslaved to immoral desires.

For example, among homosexuals, same-sex attraction is so strong that they wrongfully assume it is a natural and therefore legitimate expression of their identity, which in their mind justifies their same-sex orientation. But as stated earlier, whenever the object of one's desire is for what God forbids, the desire itself is sinful. Paul categorizes it as "the desire of the flesh . . . . For the flesh sets its desire against the Spirit" (Gal. 5:16b–17). And as demonstrated in our previous exposition of Romans 1:24, Paul uses the term "lust" (*epithumeō*) to describe evil cravings, immoral desires, and a yearning for what God forbids. As Jesus stated in Matthew 5:28, ". . . everyone who looks at a woman with *lust* for her has already committed adultery with her in his heart" (emphasis mine), making lust a manifestation of an immoral heart rooted in our sinful nature. "For out of the heart come evil thoughts, murders, adulteries, fornications, thefts, false witness, slanders. These are the things which defile the man" (Matt. 15:19–20).

So to somehow justify homosexuality on the basis of unbridled same-sex attraction directly contradicts the clear teaching of Scripture where homosexuality is condemned in the same way as "those who are lawless and rebellious . . . the ungodly and sinners . . . the unholy and profane . . . those who kill their fathers or mothers . . . murderers and immoral men and homosexuals and kidnappers and liars and perjurers, and whatever else is contrary to sound teaching, according to the glorious gospel of the blessed God" (1 Tim. 1:9–11).

Those who are truly regenerate, however, will readily acknowledge that they "formerly lived in the lusts of [their] flesh, indulging the desires of the flesh and of the mind, and were by nature children of wrath" yet the Spirit "made [them] alive together with Christ" (Eph. 2:3, 5). At the moment of our new birth, we are made new creatures in Christ, setting into motion a process of sanctification what will culminate in Christlikeness, for "that which is born of the flesh is flesh, and what which is born of the Spirit is spirit" (John 3:6; cf. John 1:13; 1 Peter 1:23). For this reason Paul says, "If anyone is in Christ, he is a new creature; the old things passed away; behold, new things have come" (2 Cor. 5:17).

Solely by the power of God's grace through the agency of His Spirit and His Word, the life of the newborn saint is characterized by overcoming the wicked influences of Satan's world system (1 John 5:4)—and this includes a newfound hatred for what he or she once loved, and a love for what he or she once hated. The Spirit plants within us new desires, loves, passions, inclinations, beliefs, and values so that we are able to "cleanse ourselves from all defilement of flesh and spirit, perfecting holiness in the fear of God" (2 Cor. 7:1).

What a magnificent thing it is to observe the Spirit of God change not only behaviors, but also the very desires of a person's heart—a transformation every believer can affirm, for "we too all formerly lived in the lusts of our flesh, indulging the desires of the flesh and of the mind, and were by nature children of wrath, even as the rest" (Eph. 2:3). And even for the homosexual, I have seen it on many occasions—a man doesn't begin to have sexual desires for other women in general, for that would be immoral—but he will have a godly desire for the wife that God provides for him (Prov. 5:18–19).

This is the supernatural power and promise of the gospel that manifests God's love for sinners and His desire to bless those who bow to the authority of His truth. And this is why Jesus prayed, "Sanctify them in the truth; Your word is truth" (John 17:17).

4

·············

The Christian's Assembly

Christ's Church Under Siege

"Not everyone who says to Me, 'Lord, Lord,' will enter the kingdom of heaven, but he who does the will of My Father who is in heaven will enter.'"

Matthew 7:21

In the providence of God, I encountered a friend I hadn't seen in several years, a man I considered a brother in Christ. It happened to be during the height of the 2020 presidential campaign season where emotions ran hot on both ends of the political spectrum—which quickly became evident in our conversation. Although he knew my well-documented positions on social/moral issues as a conservative evangelical pastor, he immediately launched into a vicious tirade against the incumbent president Donald Trump and anyone who might support his policies. With severe animus and well-rehearsed rhetoric, he attacked his "racist, homophobic, transphobic, misogynistic, and xenophobic policies." It was obvious my friend had gone full blown "woke." It was also obvious he was baiting me, itching for a fight.

After listening to him for a while, I pushed back ever so kindly and gently. But when I did, his tone got increasingly shrill. He eventually began to rebuke me "for not standing with the oppressed against systemic racism." When I asked him to point me to any reliable research to validate his claims of "systemic racism" (knowing there is none), he was unable to do so, and quickly retorted, "You don't see it because you're white, you're privileged, in fact, all white people are racists." Since his blood was up, I knew reasonable dialogue wasn't an option, so I just let him talk. He continued to lecture me on Critical Race Theory and why I was wrong not to support Black Lives Matter, including the LGBTQ agenda. He then said, "Brother, your Christianity isn't truly Christian because you're not demonstrating the love of Christ who said we should love our neighbor"—a popular but misleading falsehood that exalts God's love in order to mitigate His holiness—a holiness that requires all sin to be punished.

But finally, when he told me "the goal of the gospel and the purpose of the church includes the promotion of social justice." I leaned into him and said, "Enough! I will hear no more of this. What you're saying is a gross misrepresentation of the gospel and the purpose of the church. It dishonors Christ and His Word, and I categorically reject everything you just said. Some of your positions are morally reprehensible in God's eyes, even blasphemous." And with that, I suggested we change the subject, which we did, at least for a few minutes. Then he excused himself and, sadly, we parted company, maybe for good.

Oppressive Orthodoxy

To be sure, the church is under siege. Increasingly we see how anyone who holds to historic evangelical orthodoxy is considered an oppressive bigot, racist, and homophobe, out of touch with reality and bereft of Christian love. And this is not merely the settled conviction of the average unregenerate American; you expect those who live in darkness to be blind to the truth (1 Cor. 2:14). But what is truly remarkable is how *the same charges are being made by prominent voices in evangelicalism.* Unlike Jesus who refused to be worshipped by the self-righteous mob who saw Him as their social justice Messiah who would free them from Rome and give them free food and political power, they cave in to the mob and say, "Oh yeah, Jesus is all about that, too; and so are we!" To say otherwise would result in the same outcome as Jesus had when He exposed the fickle faith of His followers and their utter dependence upon His sovereign grace for salvation: "As a result of this many of His disciples withdrew and were not walking with Him anymore" (John 6:66).

For a professing Christian to hold views that are so blatantly unbiblical really calls into question not only what it means to be *evangelical*, but also what it means to be a *Christian*. Like many other pastors, I find myself cringing when I say I'm an *evangelical Christian* when in fact I have very little in common with many who claim the same. And some are so far beyond the pale I have no doubt they are utterly lost. For example, the Democratic National Convention featured as one of their speakers a person who, according to most people, would fall under the category of "evangelical." This person's name is J Mai, who identifies as a "Black-Vietnamese, transgender nonbinary/gender transcendent mermaid Queen-King," who recently became a "licensed minister in the Progressive National Baptist Church." J Mai advocates abolishing the police, ICE, and prisons. "J received their Bachelors in Sociology and Women, Gender, Sexuality Studies at Wake

Forest University and is currently working towards a Masters in Divinity at Wake Forest University School of Divinity."[32] This is so exceedingly sad; it is evidence of a person who has been "[given] over to a depraved mind, to do those things which are not proper" (Rom. 1:28)—as are those who embrace such insanity. Now I realize, this is a shocking example. But what is not shocking is to see how many so-called evangelicals see no problem with this. Instead, biblical Christians who are utterly appalled by such sacrilege offend them! The true church of Jesus Christ has nothing in common with this kind of false religion, "for what partnership have righteousness and lawlessness, or what fellowship has light with darkness? Or what harmony has Christ with Belial, or what has a believer in common with an unbeliever?" (2 Cor. 6:14–15). Whenever I encounter the growing number of blasphemous beliefs and practices in ostensibly evangelical circles, the apostle Paul's warnings in Ephesians 5:11–17 come to mind:

> Do not participate in the unfruitful deeds of darkness, but instead even expose them; for it is disgraceful even to speak of the things which are done by them in secret. But all things become visible when they are exposed by the light, for everything that becomes visible is light. For this reason it says, "Awake, sleeper, and arise from the dead, and Christ will shine on you." Therefore be careful how you walk, not as unwise men but as wise, making the most of your time, because the days are evil. So then do not be foolish, but understand what the will of the Lord is.

The spectrum of heresy within the ranks of evangelicalism is so vast it would fill numerous volumes, and upon completion, it would require a full-time staff to record the new ones that appear every day. Like fruit flies on a rotten banana, new heresies emerge daily. For example,

> Recent surveys reveal that a large percentage of people who self-identify as "evangelical" do not understand even the most basic principles of gospel truth. In a recent poll of self-styled

32   https://tennesseestar.com/2020/08/21/dnc-panel-features-mermaid-queen-king-who-calls-for-the-abolition-of-ice-police-and-prisons/

evangelicals, 52 percent said they reject the concept of absolute truth; 61 percent do not read the Bible daily; 75 percent believe people are basically good; 48 percent believe salvation can be earned by good works; 44 percent believe the Bible does not condemn abortion; 43 percent believe Jesus may have sinned; 78 percent believe Jesus is the first being created by God; 46 percent believe the Holy Spirit is a force rather than a Person; 40 percent believe lying is morally acceptable in certain circumstances; 34 percent accept same-sex marriage as consistent with biblical teaching; 26 percent reject Scripture as God's Word; and 50 percent say church attendance is not necessary. Most of those views are categorically incompatible with saving faith. In other words, many who self-identify as evangelicals are not believers at all."[33]

When the Church Caves in to the Culture

As unbelievable as all this may seem, this is where Satan's deceptions have taken our country, and even certain quarters of the "church." This is what happens when the gospel is distorted and ignored. This is what happens when the church caves in to the culture. As I have written elsewhere,

> We now live in a postmodern age that poses many unique threats to the evangelical church. Many pastors admit they are in crisis because of this. Evangelicalism—once defined by its commitment to doctrines and practices of the Protestant Reformation—has now become an amorphous spiritual movement whose only connection to the historic Christian faith is what is written on the doctrinal statement of individual churches . . . . Unfortunately, most evangelicals believe the most effective means to reach this postmodern world for Christ is for the church to become more attractive and relevant to the culture. It must reinvent itself, adjust its gospel message, be less dogmatic, more therapeutic, tolerant, and entertaining. It must pander to the culture, take up its social causes, even conform to it, but never oppose it.

---

33 https://blog.tms.edu/is-the-evangelical-movement-really-evangelical

Others argue, as I do . . . that such a position is totally foreign to Scripture and therefore mitigates the power and blessing of God. Moreover, because God is not even remotely like us, it is foolish to try to make Him part of us. His nature and attributes are infinitely beyond our ability to even imagine. His greatness and holiness are outside the bounds of our thoughts and ways. Therefore, He cannot be adapted to fit into our world—a world he has gone to such great lengths to save us out of and will one day destroy.

Though hideously offensive to the culture, God is concerned with only one thing: *His glory*, which is revealed most vividly in the person and work of His beloved Son, the Lord Jesus Christ, who died vicariously to save sinners. Because of this, His church is to be singularly focused on the gospel and His promise to save all who turn from sin and trust in Christ as Savior and Lord.

Furthermore, by its very nature the church is radically different from anything in culture. It is an outpost of a celestial kingdom the world cannot comprehend. It is made up of alien people whose citizenship is in heaven—people who have received a Word from another realm and who long to leave this earth at God's appointed time. So when Christians meet together to worship, they do so because an unfathomably glorious God has summoned them to worship Him and hear from Him, making their worship services an otherworld experience—a gathering where God speaks through the stammering lips of divinely appointed men, and where sacraments are administered in remembrance of Christ, keeping His worshippers in a state of breathless adoration.

In light of this biblical worldview, instead of reinventing the church to make it relevant . . . we must recapture the essence of the New Testament church whose spiritual authenticity can be seen most clearly in the Protestant church of the Reformation."[34]

---

34   David A. Harrell, *Seven Key Principles for Effective Ministry: Nurturing Thriving Churches in a Postmodern Culture* (Wapwallopen, Pennsylvania: Shepherd Press, 2019), 14–15.

Regeneration and Self-Deception

Spiritual apostasy within the ranks of evangelicalism has caused it to be on a precipitous decline for many years, especially since its partnering with theological liberalism in the nineteenth century—a system that essentially denies the inspiration and authority of Scripture and argues that Christianity is more defined by feelings and experience than adherence to certain doctrines. As a result, the very definition of a Christian has become so blurred that virtually anyone who has fond feelings for the benevolent aspects of the teachings of Christ can be considered a Christian. Historically, this spawned the ecumenical movement that believes Christianity has nothing to do with embracing fundamental biblical truths essential to salvation, but is rather defined by people who love God and love one another. While commitment to unity might appear on the surface to be a commendable cause, unity at the expense of truth is a damning deception. As Iain Murray states,

> Liberalism has had all the marks of the false prophet. It promised a great growth in light and Christian influence for the nations where it was adopted. Instead there has been spiritual desolation. This is exactly what we who believe Scripture should have expected.[35]

Wherever the essential doctrines of soteriology are discarded as the ancient relics of fundamental obscurantists who cause unnecessary division, the true gospel will be replaced by a false gospel and the church will be populated with unbelievers. We all know people who affirm the gospel and yet remain strangers to its saving and sanctifying power. This was true of a good friend of mine who was saved out of a lifetime of regular church attendance in a liberal church where he never heard the true gospel. He became gloriously saved and has now been a faithful pastor for number of years. Here's what he said:

> Having lived most of my life in the so-called "Bible Belt," I have met and known scores of people who profess to be

---

35 Iain H. Murray, *Evangelicalism Divided: A Record of Crucial Change in the Years 1950 to 2000* (Edinburgh: The Banner of Truth Trust, 2000), 313.

Christians, yet in their daily lives have been indistinguishable from those who have never made such a profession. In fact, I myself used to be such a person. I have lived both sides and seen the fallacy of one and the truth of the other.

Such people as I once was rarely read their Bibles, much less know them. They take no delight in talking about the things of the Lord. Their lifestyles are as worldly and self-indulgent as their incomes will allow, and oftentimes more than they will allow. Their minds are set on and preoccupied with earthly things. In their dress they take their cues from the culture, or are driven by personal preference rather than biblical principles, and are just as immodest, provocative, ostentatious, and sensual as the world.

They allow the culture to dictate the standard of modesty and morality, and what is appropriate and inappropriate. They watch the same ungodly movies, listen to the same music, are influenced by and follow the same fads and trends, and reflect the same values, priorities, thinking, and reasoning of the culture. Their speech is often coarse and profane. Their social media platforms are shallow, vain, self-promotional, compliment-seeking, and narcissistic. They have no devotion or love for spiritual truths and biblical principles, especially if they contradict some preference or presupposition, or require an alteration in their thinking, values, beliefs, and lifestyles, and to forsake some cherished lust and sin.

Their giving to the work of the Lord is sporadic, self-serving, and minimal at best, with virtually no inconvenience to their overall lifestyle. They are not only utterly incapable of discerning truth from error, the clean from the unclean, the holy from the profane, and the fruit that is from the spirit of the world from the fruit that is of the Spirit of God, but they are completely indifferent toward them. They can listen to what is good and true, and to what is bad and heretical, without any discrimination.

But for all of this they are quite certain they will go to heaven when they die. If you ask them what is the basis for this confidence, they will tell you that many years ago they accepted Jesus as their Savior and invited Him into their heart, and "once saved, always saved" is their comfort and assurance. But the sign and evidence that someone is truly regenerate is not some empty prattling about how secure they are once they made a profession of faith, but "that though you were slaves of sin, you became obedient from the heart to that form of teaching to which you were committed" (Rom. 6:17).[36]

Perhaps the most chilling statement in the Bible is recorded in Matthew 7:21 where Jesus says, "Not everyone who says to Me, 'Lord, Lord,' will enter the kingdom of heaven." What a dire warning to the masses of people who claim to be Christians but are not. What a horrifying climax to a life of self-deception when those who have professed Christ with their lips but not with their life will stand before Jesus Christ as their Judge and Executioner, but not as their Savior and "Lord" as they claimed. A day when "the One who has been appointed by God as Judge of the living and the dead" (Acts 10:42) will strip away the external robes of hypocrisy and expose the naked truth of a soul that was "Christian" in name only.

Jesus' frightening prediction should cause everyone who calls Jesus "Lord" to make a careful, unbiased, and brutally honest evaluation of his or her heart. As the apostle Paul warned, "Test yourselves to see if you are in the faith; examine yourselves! Or do you not recognize this about yourselves, that Jesus Christ is in you—unless indeed you fail the test?" (2 Cor. 13:5).

The Broad and the Narrow Way

In Matthew 7, Jesus begins to address these dangers by cautioning believers to use righteous discernment when judging others (vv. 1–2; cf. John 7:24). Then He warns of the hypocrite who is prone to see the speck in another man's eye but not the log in his own (vv. 3–4)—a reference to professing Christians who cannot perceive who they really are. Jesus says in Matthew 6:22–23, "The lamp of the body is the eye; if therefore your eye is clear, your whole body will be full of light. But if your eye is bad, your whole

---

36   John Fast: https://hilltopbiblechurch.org/2019/06/01/living-in-dangerous-times-part-13/

body will be full of darkness. If therefore the light that is in you is darkness, how great is the darkness!" Hypocrites cannot see the light of truth because the internal corruption of their very nature emanates darkness from within them, causing them to walk in darkness, which they perceive to be light.

Jesus then presses His followers to choose between two options, both claiming "This way to heaven!" First, He asks them to choose between two gates: the *narrow* and the *wide*, and then commands them to "Enter through the narrow gate: for the gate is wide and the way is broad that leads to destruction" (Matt. 7:13). The term "narrow" (*stenos*) comes from a root word meaning "to groan" and is used to describe a compressed or restrictive gate that is not entered with ease. John Nolland writes:

> Matthew has probably chosen the imagery of narrowness to suggest the constriction of one's choices involved in taking the challenge of Jesus' teaching: there is a very sharply defined mode of entry. The narrow gate throws up images of the need to make a choice which is not obvious (this is not where the crowd is going to go), to be attentive to where the gate is located, perhaps to experience the discomfort of squeezing through a narrow space.[37]

The gate of authentic saving faith requires someone to squeeze through without the excess baggage of self-righteousness. It requires the recognition of spiritual bankruptcy, of being consumed with guilt over sin and fully aware of the judgment deserved for having violated the laws of a holy God. When a person truly comes to saving faith, he or she will experience the intense pressure of a conscious choice to renounce the old self and put on Christ—a determined, purposeful decision requiring strenuous effort. This, of course, is the opposite of the "easy-believism" and "decisionism" of altar-call revivalism where calculated and emotionally induced outward acts (like walking an aisle and repeating a prayer) are considered to be evidence of regeneration rather than a changed life.

We see the same emphasis in Jesus' response to the question,

---

37 J. Nolland, *The Gospel of Matthew: A Commentary on the Greek Text* (Grand Rapids, Michigan: W.B. Eerdmans; Carlisle, UK: Paternoster Press, 2005), 332.

"Lord, are there just a few who are being saved?" He answered, "Strive to enter the narrow door, for many, I tell you, will seek to enter and will not be able" (Luke 13:23–24). "Strive" (*agonizomai*) signifies an intense exertion against conflict, indicating that this is not a gate a person enters with ease, nor will it be a wide gate that attracts the masses. Instead, it will be a gate that one must enter deliberately with determined effort and all alone.

This is the gate of genuine conversion, entered by the overwhelmed, the helpless, the hopeless, the ones that cry out like the publican, "Have mercy upon me the sinner!" (Luke 18:13) This is the gate of *self-denial*, not *self-fulfillment*—a gate that requires a man to count the cost of discipleship, discard self-will, jettison self-righteousness, reject selfish ambitions, and become the willing slave of his Savior and King. Jesus put it this way: "If anyone wishes to come after Me, let him deny himself, and take up his cross, and follow Me. For whoever wishes to save his life shall lose it; but whoever loses his life for My sake shall find it" (Matt. 16:24–25). To "deny" literally means to renounce yourself, to be repulsed by your sin and all the ways it has corrupted your life and made God your enemy—a radical departure from the *man-centered gospel* of self-fulfillment and self-indulgence or the heretical *social justice gospel* that focuses on *how to be delivered from the social injustice of man* rather than *how to be delivered from the righteous justice of God*. Central to entering the narrow gate is a terrifying conviction of sin and a clear understanding of the message of Acts 4:12: "And there is salvation in no one else; for there is no other name under heaven that has been given among men by which we must be saved."

In addition to this, Jesus warns, "For the gate is small, and the way is narrow that leads to life, and few are those who find it" (Matt. 7:14). The reason they can't find it is because it's not the gate they're looking for; and it's certainly not the gate the masses choose to enter. Jesus went on to contrast the *narrow gate* with the *wide gate*, saying, "for the gate is wide, and the way is broad that leads to destruction, and many are those who enter by it" (Matt. 7:13). The imagery here is obvious: both the narrow and the wide gate have a sign over them saying "This Way to Heaven." But unlike the narrow gate that is *restrictive*, the wide gate is *gaping, inclusive,* and *attractive*. The idea of "striving" is wholly unnecessary in the wide gate; there's no need for conscious, strenuous effort; there's no need for groaning, or crying out for mercy. And the "wide . . . way" is the easy way—the way of the world, the way of the unregenerate.

Widening the Gate

Many modern-day pastors who are bent on attracting "seekers" have learned how to market the wide gate by defining sin in such a way that virtually no one could be offended, and thus eliminate the need for genuine repentance and regeneration. The essence of their definition of sin is basically this: *Sin includes all those things we think and do that rob us of fellowship with God and steal away the happiness He wants us to enjoy.* The good news of the gospel is then reduced to nothing more than *God loving us so much that He sent His Son to save us from our unhappiness.* But describing sin apart from the offended righteousness of God is not just irresponsible, it is damning. Apart from an understanding of man's condemnation that evokes the wrath of God, the gospel is no gospel at all.

This is the sad legacy of the consumer-driven mindset of evangelical pragmatism that makes the *gospel a product* and the *preacher a salesman*—a concept totally foreign to Scripture. As you might expect, the salesman must make the product appealing to the consumer by presenting it in an atmosphere of entertainment and removing any offense that might prevent the sale. But when the solemnity of the eternal destiny of people's souls is obscured by amusement, and the offense of the cross is removed to overcome resistance, the *appealing* gospel becomes a *different* gospel that damns both those who embrace it and those who preach it (Gal. 1:8). For this reason, Paul said to the Corinthians, "I determined to know nothing among you except Jesus Christ, and Him crucified" (1 Cor. 2:4). And though it was "to Jews a stumbling block and to Gentiles foolishness" (1 Cor. 1:23), he knew his uncompromising proclamation was the only truth that could save, causing him to say, "My message and my preaching were not in persuasive words of wisdom, but in demonstration of the Spirit and of power" (1 Cor. 2:4).

When the average postmodern unbeliever hears a modified gospel presented by a false teacher who is intent on overcoming resistance—as if he, not God, is sovereign over salvation—the sinner has no basis to grasp the terrifying reality that "the wrath of God abides on him" (John 3:36). Instead, he will respond as follows (consistent with numerous conversations I have had with people in this regard):

> Yeah, if God is real, I suppose I am guilty of ignoring Him. I don't think about God very much, and I love lots of things more than God. So to that extent, I suppose I am living in prideful rebellion. And yes, I have fallen just like the whole Satan analogy—just look at all the junk in my life. Relationships are messed up. My marriage is boring. My finances are a wreck. I hate my job. I basically feel as though my life is going nowhere fast. For sure, I need to be saved from all this stuff. Maybe God is the answer to my unhappiness, my lack of success, my negative emotions, and my lack of purpose and direction in life. I'm just glad God loves me just the way I am, because I'm not sure I could ever change. I am what I am. And I'm not sure why Jesus had to come and die for me (assuming all that's true), but I'm glad He did, I guess. I sure don't get all that stuff about the Father killing His Son—so much for a loving God. But I'm told I have to accept that stuff by faith, so I guess I will. Nothing else seems to be working. I suppose Jesus died on the cross so He could demonstrate what selfless love is all about. Anyway, I want to take advantage of anything God may have to offer to make my life better. So I think I'll accept Jesus as my personal Savior and see what happens.

Moralistic Therapeutic Deism

Perhaps one of the most graphic manifestations of this kind of unregenerate pseudo-Christian thinking can be seen in the typical "Christian" teenager—a tragedy that also dominates virtually every acre of the landscape of Protestant evangelicalism. Christian Smith and his fellow researchers with the National Study of

Youth and Religion at the University of North Carolina at Chapel Hill observed the essence of this danger after conducting more than 3,000 interviews with American adolescents to determine their religious beliefs. There they discovered a deception they identified as "Moralistic Therapeutic Deism," a concept summarized in *Soul Searching: The Religious and Spiritual Eyes of American Teenagers* by Christian Smith with Melinda Lundquist Denton.[38] According to these researchers, Moralistic Therapeutic Deism consists of beliefs like these:

1. "A god exists who created and ordered the world and watches over human life on earth."
2. "God wants people to be good, nice, and fair to each other, as taught in the Bible and by most world religions."
3. "The central goal of life is to be happy and to feel good about oneself."
4. "God does not need to be particularly involved in one's life except when God is needed to resolve a problem."
5. "Good people go to heaven when they die." That, in sum, is the creed to which much adolescent faith can be reduced. . . . When it came to the most crucial questions of faith and beliefs, many adolescents responded with a shrug and "whatever."

As a matter of fact, the researchers. . . found that American teenagers are incredibly inarticulate about their religious beliefs, and most are virtually unable to offer any serious theological understanding. As Smith reports, "To the extent that the teens we interviewed did manage to articulate what they understood and believed religiously, it became clear that most religious teenagers either do not really comprehend what their own religious traditions say they are supposed to believe, or they do understand it and simply do not care to believe it. Either way, it is apparent that most religiously affiliated U.S. teens are not particularly interested in espousing and upholding the beliefs of their faith traditions, or that their communities of faith are failing in attempts to educate their youth, or both."

---

38 http://www.christianpost.com/news/moralistic-therapeutic-deism-the-new-amercian-religion.html

As the researchers explained, "For most teens, nobody has to do anything in life, including anything to do with religion. 'Whatever' is just fine, if that's what a person wants."[39]

What a radically different attitude and response to that of the tax collector in Luke 18 who, when confronted with his sin, was so overwhelmed with guilt and unworthiness that he "was even unwilling to lift up his eyes to heaven, but was beating his breast, saying, 'God, be merciful to me, the sinner!'" (v. 13). This is certainly evidence of regeneration that will yield the fruits of genuine repentance. What a blessed thing it is to behold the Holy Spirit awakening souls to the truth of their sin and their Savior! And when fully awakened, such people will forsake everything to enter in through the narrow gate of genuine repentance.

In Luke 16:16, Jesus warned that when "the gospel of the kingdom of God is preached . . . everyone is forcing his way into it." This denotes a vigorous, forceful pressing into the kingdom. Jesus expanded upon this concept warning that "from the days of John the Baptist until now the kingdom of heaven suffers violence, and violent men take it by force" (Matt. 11:12). There, Jesus emphasized that, despite the world's relentless opposition to the kingdom of God, it will never be subdued by the wickedness of men or the power of Satan. And those who, by the power of regenerating grace that energizes faith, see their sin and love the Savior will forcefully press their way into the kingdom, even if it costs them their life.

So Jesus presses His followers to choose between two options both claiming "This way to heaven!" They must choose between two gates: the *narrow* and the *wide*, and between two ways: the *narrow* and the *broad*. The world will hate those who enter in through the narrow, but love those who chose the wide. Saints will suffer on the narrow way, but those who are "Christians" in name only will fit right in with the rest of the unregenerate on the broad way. True believers will *serve Christ* on the narrow way, but the unsaved will *serve self* and "[their] father the devil" (John 8:44) on the broad way.

Sadly, much of the church today is made up of *wide gate, broad*

---

39   Ibid.

way "Christians" who are externally religious, and even claim to be "born again," but who have no saving understanding of the true gospel and have not wholeheartedly embraced Christ in repentant faith. For example, one in four born-again "Christians" embraces universalist beliefs when it comes to salvation, according to a Barna analysis of trend data. Twenty-five percent of born-again Christians said all people are eventually saved or accepted by God. A similar proportion, 26 percent, said a person's religion does not matter because all faiths teach the same lessons. And an even higher proportion, 40 percent, of born-again Christians said they believe Christians and Muslims worship the same God. Barna defined universalism as the belief that all human beings will eventually be saved after death. The California-based research and polling firm defines born-again Christians as people who have made "a personal commitment to Jesus Christ that is still important in their life today, and who believe they will go to heaven after death because they confessed their sins and accepted Jesus Christ as their savior."[40] But sadly, given the heresy many believe, they will one day learn otherwise.

The Dire Warning

In light of this, Jesus offers the most horrifying prediction ever made concerning the masses of people who fall prey to self-deception and believe they have been raised from spiritual death to spiritual life and reconciled God through faith in His Son, the Lord Jesus Christ, when in fact, they have not. He said, "Not everyone who says to Me, 'Lord, Lord,' will enter the kingdom of heaven, but he who does the will of My Father who is in heaven will enter" (Matt. 7:21). What a terrifying thought! This is one of the most sobering passages in Scripture—one that describes the horrifying climax of self-deception. Here the masquerade of the *many* who entered the *wide gate* and traveled the *broad way* is exposed.

The prophetic lament, "Lord, Lord," that Jesus describes is haunting—one that indicates they will have a perceived zeal and devotion to Christ. They will honestly believe that their profession

---

40   http://www.christianpost.com/news/many-born-again-christians-hold-universalist-view-barna-finds-49883/#MOf0DZqyPXOroJUh.99

and conduct were certain proof that they were followers of Christ. It is important to note that Jesus is not necessarily referring to heretics, agnostics, atheists, apostates, or pagans, but to those who profess faith in Him. They will call Him Lord. But obviously, not all who *profess* Him actually *possess* Him. A man's profession alone is meaningless unless it is validated by a selfless life devoted to Christ—the inevitable manifestation of the new birth! True believers are "[known] by their fruits" (Matt. 7:20), not by their profession of allegiance to Christ. For this reason, Jesus went on to say, "Not everyone who says to Me, 'Lord, Lord,' will enter the kingdom of heaven; *but he who does the will of My father who is in heaven*" (v. 21; emphasis mine).

Their ignorance of this most fundamental truth can be seen in the contrast of Jesus' use of the words "says" rather than "does" in verse 21. Here the old adage "What we do speaks louder than words" is most fitting. To be sure, talk is cheap. Therefore, obedience is the only reliable indicator of one's faith in Christ. What validates spiritual rebirth and genuine saving faith is *doing the will of the Father* (Matt. 7:21).

Now, it is important to point out that we don't *earn* our salvation by faith *plus* works. That is the damning heresy of a false gospel, like we see in the Roman Catholic church that teaches justification is a result of *faith plus works; grace plus merit; through Christ plus other mediators; by Scripture plus tradition; for the glory of God plus Mary and other saints.* This is why there was a Protestant Reformation (1517–1648). The Reformers taught the true gospel whose basic theological principles are summarized in the *Five Solas* (five Latin phrases or slogans):

- *Sola Fide,* by faith alone;
- *Sola Scriptura,* by Scripture alone;
- *Solus Christus,* through Christ alone;
- *Sola Gratia,* by grace alone;
- *Soli Deo Gloria,* glory to God alone.

The true gospel teaches that works don't *earn* salvation; they *prove* it (James 2:17). Jesus said, "If you abide in My Word, then you are truly disciples of Mine" (John 8:31). Works are never the *root* of justification by faith; they are the *fruit* of it. The apostle John writes,

> The one who says, "I have come to know Him," and does not keep His commandments, is a liar, and the truth is not in him; but whoever keeps His word, in him the love of God has truly been perfected. By this we know that we are in Him; the one who says he abides in Him ought himself to walk in the same manner as He walked.
> (1 John 2:3–6)

This describes a life pattern of Christlike obedience to the will of God energized by the miracle of the new birth; otherwise, ". . . faith, if it has no works, is dead, being by itself" (James 2:17).

Once again, in Matthew 7, Jesus makes it clear that the majority of those who profess Him as Lord are *self-deceived*, proven by lives that did not demonstrate their professed allegiance to Him. Unlike the *few*, the *many* "do not do the will of the Father who is in heaven"—a sheer impossibility apart from the regenerating work of the Holy Spirit. They professed Christ with their lips but not with their lives, because they were still spiritually "dead in [their] trespasses and sins" (Eph. 2:1).

The Dubious Defense

Jesus went on to describe the *dubious defense* of the self-deceived—those who masqueraded as His disciples by performing religious works and making orthodox declarations of faith without any heartfelt love for Christ or commitment to obey His will. In perhaps the most alarming words in all of Scripture, Jesus describes the terrifying dialogue in this coming hour of judgment, saying,

> Many will say to Me on that day, "Lord, Lord, did we not prophesy in Your name, and in Your name cast out demons, and in Your name perform many miracles?" And then I will declare to them, "I never knew you; depart from Me, you who practice lawlessness."
> (Matt. 7:22–23)

The eschatological scene is one of unspeakable incredulity and terror. The damned are dumfounded! They can't believe they're standing before the Lord Jesus Christ not as their *Savior* and *Lord*, but as their *Judge* and *Executioner*. In desperation the "many" will plead their case, but to no avail; and in an effort to demonstrate their submission to His sovereign rule, they will address Him with a perfunctory, "Lord, Lord." They will argue their case enthusiastically by supplying outward signs of devotion to Christ and His church, including what they considered to be miraculous gifts of the Holy Spirit such as *prophecies, exorcisms,* and various other kinds of *miracles* (v. 22)—counterfeit signs and wonders that can be fabricated by human chicanery and demonic influence (*cf.* Acts 19:13–16; Rev. 13:13–14). But the penetrating eye of divine omniscience will see the truth. Then Jesus will say, "I never knew you," indicating that even those with the most sincere profession of faith will be sent away to destruction if they entered the *wide gate* and traversed the *broad way* of the worldly masses who were Christian in name only.

What a contrast to the *narrow gate* that demands self-denial and repentance produced by regeneration—the gate of genuine saving faith that requires people to give up all that they *are* and *have* to follow Christ. This is the gate of the "few" who are "humble and contrite of spirit, and who tremble at [His] word" (Isa. 66:2); those who "mourn" over their sin (Matt. 5:4) and "hunger and thirst for righteousness" (Matt. 5:6); those who seek the one true Lord with all their heart (Jer. 29:13).

But the "Christless" Christians of the *wide gate* and the *broad way* will be those who served a god of their own liking and making—one that appealed to their fallen flesh, one they were convinced would accept them on their terms. Therefore, what they *say* will not match what they *did*—an accusation consistent with Jesus' rebuke in Luke 6:46 when He said: "Why do you call Me, 'Lord, Lord,' and do not do what I say?" This will be the dreadful end of the unregenerate that were never raised from spiritual death to spiritual life (John 3:6). John MacArthur described it this way:

> The repentant life will be a changed life. The primary message of John's first epistle is that the truly redeemed life will

manifest itself in a transformed life, in which confession of sin (1:8–10), obedience to God's will (2:4–6), love of God's other children (2:9–11; 3:16–17), and practice of righteousness (3:4–10) are normal and habitual. "By this is My Father glorified, that you bear much fruit, and so prove to be My disciples" (John 15:8). Anything less is damning demon-faith (James 2:19) that is orthodox but fruitless.[41]

Sadly, the absence of spiritual fruit is one of the most defining characteristics of modern evangelicalism. While worldliness and doctrinal compromise are major contributors to this barrenness, the greatest corruptor is the massive number of unregenerate professing Christians who make up the church today. It is no wonder the church has so little spiritual authority and influence on the culture. Jesus warned of this when He said,

> You are the salt of the earth; but if the salt has become tasteless, how can it be made salty again? It is no longer good for anything, except to be thrown out and trampled under foot by men. You are the light of the world. A city set on a hill cannot be hidden; nor does anyone light a lamp and put it under a basket, but on the lampstand, and it gives light to all who are in the house. Let your light shine before men in such a way that they may see your good works, and glorify your Father who is in heaven.
> (Matt. 5:13–16)

Instead of being "the salt of the earth" that slows down the decay and corruption of society and preserves that which is true and holy, "the salt has become tasteless," unable to oppose corruption, unable to influence society as a moral antiseptic, unable to provide a taste of godliness in a world that knows so little of it. Unfortunately, such a church is "no longer good for anything, except to be thrown out and trampled under foot by men" (v. 13)—and that is precisely what we see happening to the church today. Furthermore, instead of the church being "the light of the world" that illumines the darkness with the dazzling

---

41 John F. MacArthur, *Matthew 1–7: The MacArthur New Testament Commentary* (Chicago, Illinois: Moody Publishers, 1985), 454.

light of the gospel and the radiant beams of righteousness—the very purpose of our redemption—it now contributes to the darkness with its prosperity-cult charlatans, entertainment-driven ministries, and culturally driven gospel distortions that are purposefully *humanitarian* rather than *redemptive*.

The pseudo-Christianity in our culture continues to be fertile soil for the seeds of depravity to germinate and grow into a harvest of unimaginable and unrestrained moral degeneracy in our country. Satanic lies and diabolical political movements are now so rampant in the United States of America that it has become obvious to any rational observer that our nation is descending into an abyss of lawless anarchy from which there may be no recovery. And much of the blame can be placed on false teachers and undiscerning pastors who refuse to confront sin and its effects with the only truth that can save, like the wicked leaders of ancient Judah that God rebuked through His servant Jeremiah saying,

> "They have healed the brokenness of My people superficially, saying, 'Peace, peace,' but there is no peace. Were they ashamed because of the abomination they have done? They were not even ashamed at all; they did not even know how to blush. Therefore they shall fall among those who fall; at the time that I punish them, they shall be cast down," says the LORD.
> (Jer. 6:14–15)

The Damning Sentence

I cannot imagine a statement that can even remotely compare to Jesus' horrifying pronouncement, "I never knew you; depart from Me, you who practice lawlessness" (Matt. 7:23). Jesus' use of the word "knew" (*ginōskō*) was related to a Hebrew idiom denoting an intimate, loving relationship, often used to describe marital intimacy (see Gen. 4:1, 17; etc.; where "had relations" is literally translated "knew," as in the KJV). We see this in Jesus' declaration: "My sheep hear My voice, and I know them" (John 10:27).

The Lord of the church to whom has been given "all authority

. . . in heaven and on earth" (Matt. 28:18) will see through the external religious veneer of the hypocrites who entered the *wide gate* and traveled the *broad way* of the *many* rather than the *few* and say, "Depart from Me, you who practice lawlessness" (Matt. 7:23b)—the grammar of the phrase indicating continuous, habitual actions. And indeed, this is the heart pattern of the unregenerate. Their life-dominating motivations and their secret desires are self-willed and rebellious against God, despite their outward religiosity. Later we read our Lord's haunting words: "that house . . . fell—and great was its fall" (Matt.7:27b).

Such will be the damning sentence of the unregenerate who professed Him with their lips, but not with their lives, those who "did not receive the love of the truth so as to be saved" (2 Thess. 2:10). Although God is unmistakably clear, America hates God's loving invitation to come to him in repentant in faith and be saved. Worse yet—and this is truly heartbreaking—many professing evangelicals who are Christian in name only share the same sentiment. Because they seek the favor of men rather than God they "distort the gospel of Christ" and "preach . . . a gospel contrary to what [they] received" from God, they are therefore "accursed" (Gal. 1:8–10). With utmost love and forthright compassion, I offer this warning from the writer of Hebrews: "It is a terrifying thing to fall into the hands of the living God" (Heb. 10:31).

5

·············

The Christian's Adversary

The Deceptive Enemy

Be of sober spirit, be on the alert. Your adversary, the devil,
prowls around like a roaring lion, seeking someone to devour.

1 Peter 5:8

An article caught my eye not long ago. It was entitled, "All People Are Holy": The Theology of Alexandria Ocasio-Cortez"—a radical leftist U.S. Representative for New York's fourteenth congressional district commonly known as "AOC." The author of the article, Morgan Guyton, is the director of the NOLA Wesley Foundation, which is the United Methodist campus ministry at Tulane and Loyola University in New Orleans, LA; he is also the author of *How Jesus Saves the World from Us:12 Antidotes To Toxic Christianity*. In his commentary, he showered praise on AOC and affirmed her theology saying,

> Alexandria Ocasio-Cortez summarized one of my core religious convictions in a speech given on February 27, 2020 in a hearing about "religious freedom." She said: "I know and it is part of my faith that all people are holy and all people are sacred. Unconditionally." It's the kind of theological declaration that I would have mocked as unserious pedestrian liberalism when I was an evangelical, but the beauty of her sincere conviction utterly pierced my heart when I watched her speech. To say that all people are holy is the polar opposite of the core evangelical doctrine that all people are totally depraved by nature. And yet I think it's an absolutely Christian thing to believe. . . . It's such a different Christianity when the first thing we say is "All people are holy." And instead of worrying about correcting other people, we decide to act as though God thinks they're gorgeously fabulous exactly as they are. Honestly I think that when I live with that conviction, I do a better job of correcting my own sin along the way. If Alexandria Ocasio-Cortez's faith is the future of American Christianity, then that's a faith worth fighting for.[42]

Pelagianism: The Theology of Revolution

To say Ocasio-Cortez and the progressive journalist espouse Christian heresy would be an understatement. If "all people are holy," there would be no need for a Savior, which, of course, is

42 https://www.patheos.com/blogs/mercynotsacrifice/2020/06/29/all-people-are-holy-the-theology-of-alexandria-ocasio-cortez/

exactly the point. Who needs a Lamb of God to take away the sins of the world if people are already holy? Who needs to be justified and reconciled to a holy God if we're all fine just the way we are? This is a tragic example of the kind of deception Satan uses to thwart the redemptive purposes of God and destroy America in the process. It is rooted in the ancient Christian heresy called Pelagianism, stemming from the fourth-century British monk Pelagius who emphasized human ability and free will rather than depravity and sinfulness. He believed the effect of Adam's sin was merely one of setting a bad example for his descendants, but it was not directly transmitted to them. Humans are not actually guilty for Adam's sin, and neither do they inherit a sinful nature from him (as Scripture teaches—see Romans 5:18–19); therefore people can obey God without the transforming power of divine grace.

AOC's theology is appealing to fallen humanity because it confirms what people already believe about themselves. Moreover, it is especially appealing to progressives because it is essential to their social agenda. *Pelagianism is the theology of revolution.* People must be seen as *deprived,* not *depraved.* For the Marxist, it's society, not a sinful nature that causes people to do bad things. Therefore it is society as a whole, not individuals that must change. And since people are inherently *good,* not *evil,* if they are given equal resources and opportunities, and if all oppressive moral, economic, and social constraints are removed, their natural goodness will flourish, and everyone will be happy. No need for a Christian Savior. No worries about divine judgment. No need for police or prisons. Once everyone's essential needs are met, and it is universally agreed that whatever a person chooses to *be* or *do* is morally acceptable and practically attainable, we will have *utopia.* Social justice at last!

Oh, one more thing. This will also require a centralized government to equally distribute resources to everyone and make sure everyone functions within the confines of what it considers to be morally acceptable and politically correct—then there will be real and lasting social justice.

Social Redeemers

....

This is truly frightening. Redemption is no longer a work of God, but a work of man. Worse yet, progressives see themselves as *social redeemers* who must grab power to promote their revolution and rid the world of capitalism and traditional religion—the root cause of all oppression, as they say.

Best-selling author, David Horowitz, a former progressive who was transformed into one of the nation's most important conservative intellectuals, recounts his childhood in a Communist household and warns against this disturbing agenda:

> In America, the war against Christians is not merely a war against an embattled religion. It is a war against an imperiled nation—a war against this nation and its founding principles: the equality of individuals and individual freedom. For these principles are indisputably Christian in origin. They are under siege because they are insurmountable obstacles to radicals' totalitarian ambition to create a new world in their image.
>
> I know this in my bones because I was born into a family of political radicals. We were a community of atheist Jews who described ourselves as "progressives" and identified our tribe as a persecuted people. . . . As progressives and world-changers, we were not interested in the fate of individual souls. Our cause was the salvation of mankind. We wanted justice for oppressed classes and races, and we looked at synagogues as reactionary institutions—houses of superstition whose prayers and preaching served to keep the oppressed in line.
>
> I eventually came to understand that my parents and their friends referred to themselves as "progressives" to hide their true faith, which was Communism. For them, Communism was the vision of a future in which the long history of social injustice would finally come to an end. When I eventually rejected this illusion, I realize that their atheistic creed was itself a form of religious faith. Their God was History, which they viewed as an inexorable march to a promised land.

> Like the religionists whom they looked down on, my parents and their leftist friends believed in a redemption, but they thought of themselves as the redeemers, not God. The real world into which their faith led them, however, was quite unexpected and the opposite of their utopian vision. A destructive fantasy had seduced them into supporting an empire whose rulers murdered millions.[43]

Once again, the grandiose delusions of social justice as defined by progressives are rooted in the lie that *humanity is basically good, not evil,* and therefore in no need of a divine Redeemer who can change a man or woman's heart to act righteously. All that is necessary is the removal of everything and everyone considered *oppressive,* and when this happens, people will no longer act in self-interest but in the interest of others. After all, as AOC says, "all people are holy and all people are sacred. Unconditionally."

But as Horowitz points out, and history confirms, this is Marxist fantasy! The kind of utopia progressives envision requires a totalitarian regime—the rule of Communism—which produces the opposite of utopia. Because in truth, human beings are sinners by nature and exceedingly selfish. We already see the rise of totalitarianism emerging in America where leftists use political power to force their agenda on everyone through any means possible.

Supreme Court Justices and the Constitution

Look no further than the battles over Supreme Court Justices and the rancor over how they interpret the Constitution. Republicans want to be governed according to an "originalist" interpretation of the Constitution that maintains the meaning it had when ratified and does not allow judges to infuse their own meaning into the text, whereas the Democratic Socialists believe the Constitution is a living document that can be interpreted in ways that may differ from the way the original drafters saw things in 1776. And this, interestingly enough, is the same kind of interpretative principle liberal theologians have used to eviscerate the true meaning

---

43   David Horowitz, *Dark Agenda: The War to Destroy Christian America* (West Palm Beach, Florida: Humanix Books, 2018), 28–29.

of the Bible and make it say whatever they want it to say.

We see the fight over judicial philosophy whenever there's a Supreme Court vacancy and a conservative judge is nominated to the court. The confirmation hearings have become so contentious that they are an embarrassment to our democracy and betray the extreme lengths liberals will go to in order to get their own way. After all, from their perspective, they're the social redeemers, the only ones who really know the truth and can save humanity. We saw this play out in Senator Ed Markey's (D., Mass.) vicious rhetoric in the 2020 confirmation process of Judge Amy Coney Barrett to the Supreme Court:

> Democrats . . . vociferously opposed Barrett's confirmation to the Court, which would give conservatives a 6–3 majority on the bench. Senator Markey on Monday criticized Barrett's adherence to Scalia's originalism. "Originalism is racist. Originalism is sexist. Originalism is homophobic. Originalism is just a fancy word for discrimination," Markey said on the Senate floor, in a line he later posted on Twitter. Markey added in his floor speech, "For originalists, LGBT stands for 'let's go back in time.'"[44]

As a baby boomer born in 1952, I have witnessed liberal elites wage war on Judeo-Christian values in an effort to gain political control, even if it meant undermining the inherent freedoms our Founding Fathers etched in the stone of the Constitution of the United States. I've repeatedly witnessed a radical leftist minority bypass the democratic process and use unelected, lifetime-tenured, liberal Supreme Court judges to legislate from the bench and compel everyone to yield to their godless ideologies.

Using tortured Constitutional arguments that stretch the bounds of reason to their breaking point and that even defy legal precedence, I have watched a handful of black-robed lawyers ban any discussion of God from public schools and bar every vestige of religion from the public square. To the horror of many, these activist judges have even ruled that a woman has a Constitutional right to kill her unwanted baby, and that homosexuals have a

---

44   https://www.nationalreview.com/news/senator-ed-markey-slams-judicial-originalism-as-racist-sexist-and-homophobic/

right to marry—decisions that are abominations in God's eyes and therefore abhorrent to Christians.

The pressure from left-wing radicals for Supreme Court Justices to embrace their Marxist agendas is far greater than the average person could ever imagine. Ted Cruz, a U.S. senator for the State of Texas who has dedicated his life to upholding the principles enshrined in the Constitution, makes this astute observation in this regard:

> Remember, if a judge changes on the bench, he or she always changes in the same way. Republican nominees only shift in one direction: they shift to the left. "Evolving" is the polite term. And it is because the pressure on a Supreme Court justice to move to the left is enormous. The press coverage consistently praises justices who vote with the left, heralding them as courageous heroes. . . . I believe there's no better predictor of whether a Supreme Court justice will remain strong and faithful to the Constitution than whether he or she has a long record of being excoriated by the press, mocked by the legal academy, and ridiculed by polite society, and holding his or her ground nonetheless. Only by looking for stoic and adamant resistance to the "Greenhouse effect" can we reliably deduce that a prospective nominee has the mettle and the fortitude to stick to his or her convictions when confronted by Washington, D.C.'s proverbial storm of locusts.[45]

Political Correctness

We also witness social redeemers exert their will on the American people through the use of *political correctness (PC)*, a clever ploy to suppress traditional religious values they deem oppressive—especially biblical Christianity—by converting Marxist economic ideology into cultural values. Indeed, *political correctness* is nothing more than *cultural Marxism* used to promote and enforce their revolutionary agenda.

---

45 Ted Cruz, *One Vote Away: How a Single Supreme Court Seat Can Change History* (Washington, D.C.: Regnery Publishing, 2020), 200–201.

Political correctness is the most powerful weapon in the arsenal of totalitarianism and can be seen most dramatically on college campuses. As conservative author Bill Lind has stated,

> The totalitarian nature of Political Correctness is revealed nowhere more clearly than on college campuses, many of which at this point are small ivy covered North Koreas, where the student or faculty member who dares to cross any of the lines set up by the gender feminist or the homosexual-rights activists, or the local black or Hispanic group, or any of the other sainted "victims" groups that PC revolves around, quickly find themselves in judicial trouble. Within the small legal system of the college, they face formal charges—some star-chamber proceeding—and punishment. That is a little look into the future that Political Correctness intends for the nation as a whole.[46]

The PC police seem to be everywhere these days, even in the workplace, ever vigilant in finding offense in every corner of our society's culture. And when they do, they *expose* and *shame* those they decide are the *oppressors* in order to *exalt* and *empower the oppressed.* Only the "woke" (those who are alert to injustice in society, especially racism) are given a voice in their politics. Everyone else is considered an oppressor and must be marginalized and silenced at all costs.

This is why so many leftists had such a visceral hatred for Donald Trump and his supporters. Trump's notorious slogan, "Make America Great Again" (MAGA) was appealing to his conservative supporters who for eight years under the Obama administration watched their beloved country degraded and destroyed by the most radical, Democratic Socialist president in American history. But the reason the radical left threw such an apoplectic fit whenever they saw a red MAGA hat is simple: *They don't want to "Make America Great Again"; they want to fundamentally change America.* They hate America! To them, America is the greatest of all oppressors—especially Christian America. So they must silence their opponents, rewrite history to fit their narrative,

---

46   https://www.academia.org/the-origins-of-political-correctness/

and implement a federal takeover of the country—and this will include, as they have stated, a *de facto* urbanization of America's suburbs. Bottom line, their goal is to utterly transform America. This is why on the eve of the November 2012 election Barack Obama proudly stated, "We are five days away from fundamentally transforming the United States of America."[47]

But we must understand, all political ideologies are rooted in a person's theology. For example, most Progressive Christians reject biblical, orthodox Christianity and see Jesus not as the Son of God who came to save sinners, but a man who came to liberate the oppressed through non-violent resistance, the quintessential model of self-sacrifice. Other cultural Marxists are either agnostics or atheists. But one thing they all have in common: *They all see themselves as the redeemers of this unjust world, creators of a new utopia that has never before existed, liberators that must usher in a new world where rational thought, scientific reason, and social justice govern humanity.* And central to their success is the abolition of all religions. Why? Because they perceive them to be nothing more than oppressive myths and superstitions that impose their ridiculous prejudices on the naïve and the ignorant.

For most cultural Marxists, religion is the root of all social problems, resulting in fantasy evils they have created, such as patriarchy, misogyny, homophobia, xenophobia, violence, racism, sexism, and bigotry—biblical Christianity being the greatest oppressor of all. And this is the kind of liberalism that defines the Democratic Party today. As David Horowitz describes it:

> [They view] American society as a system of oppressive hier-archies based on race, gender, and sexual orientation. Left-ists believe these hierarchies *must* be overthrown. Theirs is a collectivist ideology, rooted in Marxism, that is opposed to the American ideas of individual rights, individual account-ability, and individual equality.[48]

---

47 https://www.realclearpolitics.com/articles/2013/10/01/obama_transforming_america_120170.html
48 David Horowitz, *Dark Agenda: The War to Destroy Christian America* (West Palm Beach, Florida: Humanix Books, 2018), 162–3.

Misplaced Faith in Humanity

Their faith is not in the One true God who has revealed Himself in creation and in the canon of Scripture. Their faith is in *humanity*—a humanity that wants nothing to do with the God of the Bible and believes humanity is the only source of earthly redemption. Intoxicated with an inflated sense of self-worth and wisdom, smug activists assert political correctness, alienation (cancel culture), and intimidation to promote, among other things, the following: deviant sexual practices; ending the life of pre-born babies; a pro-socialist, anti-capitalist worldview; and a blurring of the borders of nations. To get themselves voted into power, its leaders incite class warfare and ethnic tensions to make people see themselves as victims. They say, "The more you feel you have been victimized, the more power you have to demand social justice."

So naturally, everyone who thinks he's a victim lines up to get his victim badge, each one hoping to cash in on the promised rewards found in reparations and other forms of wealth redistribution. This is classic Marxism. And this is at the very core of the Democratic Party in America today—a political party that must have a permanent underclass to stay in power.

It is frightening to see growing numbers of spoiled and misguided young people finding their identity in being a Social Justice Warrior, foolishly believing their postmodern ideologies (derived from man-centered philosophies like *intersectionality, radical feminism,* and *Critical Race Theory*) will usher in a glorious utopia. Like Lenin's Bolshevik revolution of 1917 that spawned the Communist Party of the Soviet Union, or the Brown Shirted hooligans of the National Socialist German Students' League of 1933 Germany, ANTIFA anarchists and Black Lives Matter thugs terrorize, loot, and burn down cities while leftist government leaders and a complicit media look on with smug satisfaction. They will stop at nothing to silence—and ultimately eradicate—those who oppose their quest for a new world order.

As stated before in this book, the authentic Christian worldview is radically different—and for good reason: *because its theology is thoroughly biblical.* But it's the opposite of the progressive "faith" illustrated by AOC's heretical statement, "I know and it is part of my faith that all people are holy and all people are sacred. Unconditionally." As we will see, the implications of that deception have both *temporal* and *eternal* consequences. The biblical view revealed by God Himself sees people as *inherently sinful in desperate need of a Savior that He alone can provide.* Unlike the Marxist social redeemers that have brought nothing but misery and death upon the world, God has provided an incarnate Redeemer who alone has accomplished our redemption through the shedding of His blood and His sacrificial death resulting in eternal life for all who believe.

To explain this, it is important to begin by refuting the Pelagian heresy expressed by the deceived congresswoman and embraced by progressives. It is my prayer that by unleashing the truth of Scripture, sinners will be converted and saints will be encouraged.

The Truth about Human Depravity

God has revealed to us a stunning reality in Scripture. One event radically altered the very nature of man and the planet on which he would live. That event was the deliberate rebellion of the first man He created, Adam. Because of Adam's sin in the garden, the entire human race was plunged into sin (Rom. 5:12) and every child is conceived in a state of sin and depravity. The psalmist put it this way: "Behold, I was brought forth in iniquity, and in sin my mother conceived me" (Ps. 51:5). Sin has penetrated and corrupted the whole of man's being (Isa. 1:6; Eph. 4:17–19), including his body (Rom. 8:10), his mind (Rom. 8:6; 1 Cor. 2:14; 4:4; Titus 1:15), his will (John 8:34; Jer. 13:23; Rom. 7:18), and his heart (Jer. 17:9).

Every person is capable of committing the very worst sins (Rom. 1:18ff; 3:10–18); and apart from the transforming grace of God in salvation, even when the unsaved individual does right, it is for motivations other than to glorify God, making such actions displeasing to Him (Matt. 6:5; 2 Tim. 3:4). Worse yet, the unsaved are utterly bereft of that love for God necessary to fulfill the most basic requirement of God's moral law to love Him supremely (Deut. 6:4; 1 John 4:7–10). God has made it clear that unregenerate people will continue to spiral downward in morality (2 Tim.

3:13; Rom. 7:23) and they have no possible means of salvation or recovery within themselves (Matt. 19:25,26; Rom. 1:18; Eph. 2:1,8).

Sin is therefore *people's innate inability to conform to the moral character and desires of God.* John says that "sin is lawlessness" (1 John 3:4), which is not only a failure to obey God's moral law, but living as if it does not exist. It is a violation of the foremost commandment to "love the Lord your God with all your heart, and with all your soul, and with all your mind" (Matt. 22:37, *cf.* v. 38).

Sin is manifested primarily in human self-will—the root cause of all sin—fueled by the cherished lies of justified rebellion against God. People prefer to obey their wills rather than God's will. This is portrayed in Scripture as "the deeds of the flesh" and it includes things like "immorality, impurity, sensuality, idolatry, sorcery, enmities, strife, jealousy, outbursts of anger, disputes, dissensions, factions, envying, drunkenness, carousing, and things like these . . . those who practice such things shall not inherit the kingdom of God" (Gal. 5:19–21). Because man is innately a slave to his sin (Rom. 6:16–20), he rejects his Creator, causing God to gradually abandon him to pursue the lusts of his heart and experience the devastating consequences of his iniquities, bringing him either to ruin or repentance (Rom. 1:24–32).

The Spin on Sin

While many liberals deny these truths outright (as in the AOC example cited earlier), many other modern-day pastors bent on attracting "seekers" tend to define sin in such a way that virtually no one could be offended. They are not told that sin is the defining characteristic of their very nature and that it is their innate inability to conform to God's moral character and desires. They are not told that all they *are* and *do* is fundamentally offensive to a holy God, rendering them guilty before His bar of justice and damned to an eternal hell, that "all have sinned and fall short of the glory of God" (Rom. 3:23), and that we must be "justified as a gift by His grace through the redemption which is in Christ Jesus, whom God displayed publicly as a propitiation in His blood through faith" (vv. 24–25). They are not warned that, because of their innate corruption, they are not only alienated from God and subject to His wrath, but are also utterly unable to save themselves.

While the biblical doctrine of sin can be heard in some religious circles, it is altogether unheard of in the public forum. Can you imagine the outrage if a Christian politician were to suggest that college curricula for public educators include a biblical course explaining our children's sinful nature and the myriad of ways it can manifest itself? The reaction would be violent. Apoplectic with rage, objectors would scream, "Every child's relentless quest for self-esteem must be guarded against such Christian lunacy." They would argue that to suggest a child's human nature is so depraved that he lives under the sentence of divine wrath is the very worst kind of child abuse; such a cruel doctrine, they would say, does irreparable damage to his fragile self-image and produces unnecessary guilt and debilitation in the human psyche.

While such a reaction is expected among non-Christians with no capacity to discern spiritual realities (1 Cor. 2:14), it is appalling to think that many professing Christians also resent these inspired truths. *There is perhaps no greater example of beguiling deceit in the church today than the distortions surrounding the doctrine of sin and the power of the gospel to save.* Unfortunately, when sin is whitewashed, the Savior becomes irrelevant.

Holiness: The Anithesis of Sin

It stands to reason that if the sinfulness of mankind is trivialized, the same fate will befall an understanding of the holiness of God. Both ends of the spectrum must be equally infinite—holiness in its transcendent purity, and sin in its vile corruption. To mitigate one is to diminish the other. Both must be held in equal tension at both ends of the spectrum of good and evil. The apostle Paul understood this. He acknowledged his deep love and respect for the holiness of God manifested in His Law when he declared, "I joyfully concur with the law of God in the inner man" (Rom. 7:22). Therefore, because of his knowledge of the Holy One, the corrupting presence and power of indwelling sin was made even more apparent to Paul, causing him to say, "But I see a different law in the members of my body, waging war against the law of my mind and making me a prisoner of the law of sin which is in my members." To this he lamented, "Wretched man that I am! Who will set me free from the body of this death?" (Rom. 7:23–24).

Every believer must grasp this simple truth: *We will only see our sin in proportion to our willingness to see the holiness of God.* Expressed differently, if we have a low view of God, we will have a high view of self. When God is small, sin is insignificant. But when we see God as He really is—the thrice-holy Lord of hosts whose glory fills the earth (Isa. 6:3)—we will respond like Isaiah and cry out, "Woe is me, for I am ruined! Because I am a man of unclean lips, and I live among a people of unclean lips; for my eyes have seen the King, the LORD of hosts" (Isa. 6:5).

To Be Set Apart

The basic meaning of *holiness* (Hebrew: *qedosh*; Greek: *hagios*) is "set apart" or "separation." Morally speaking, anything that is "holy" is set apart or separated from sin and consecrated to God. For this reason, the Old Testament speaks frequently about maintaining the distinction between things that are sacred and those considered secular or worldly. Perhaps the greatest example of this can be found in the Tabernacle where every aspect of that ancient place of worship symbolized the priority of being separate from the world. Even within the Tabernacle, God ordained that the Most Holy Place that housed the Ark of the Covenant be devoted solely to His service and separated from the sinfulness of the world by a "veil of blue and purple and scarlet material and fine twisted linen . . . made with cherubim, the work of a skillful workman" (Ex. 26:31).

Inside the Ark was the Holy Standard, the Law of Moses given on Sinai. Above the Ark on each end were golden cherubs with outstretched wings that symbolically guarded the holiness of God, and between the cherubs hovered the *shekinah* glory of God—the ineffable light of His presence, too brilliant to be seen by the fallen eyes of man. On top of the Ark was a golden lid that separated the law within from the Holy presence above, thus symbolizing that the Law had been violated and God's holiness may not be contaminated by sin.

All of this had profound implications for sinful man who desired to be reconciled to a holy God, for it was upon this lid that divine justice and grace came together symbolically once every year on the Day of Atonement. This was the holiest of days when the High Priest sprinkled the blood of an animal on that golden lid of separation. That lid was called the "Mercy Seat," the *hilasterion* in the LXX (the Septuagint or Greek translation of the Old Testament)—the Greek term that means to *appease, placate,* or *satisfy*. This was the sacrifice of atonement. The same term was used in 1 John 2:1 to describe "Jesus Christ the righteous; and He Himself is the propitiation (*hilasmos*) for our sins." Likewise we read in 1 John 4 that

> . . . God has sent His only begotten Son into the world so that we might live through Him. In this is love, not that we loved God, but that He loved us and sent His Son to be the propitiation (*hilasmos*) for our sins.
> (1 John 4:9b,10)

The amazing truth of the gospel of Christ was thereby foreshadowed in the sacrificial system. The Lord clarified this when He stated in Exodus 25:21,22:

> You shall put the mercy seat (*hilasterion*—LXX) on top of the ark, and in the ark you shall put the testimony which I will give to you. There I will meet with you; and from above the mercy seat, from between the two cherubim which are upon the ark of the testimony.

This Mercy Seat was the place where the just wrath of God was symbolically propitiated; where divine fury was appeased; where God's righteous anger was symbolically satisfied and His vengeance upon sinners placated. Only the most hardened sinner or superficial Christian could possibly contemplate such a scene and remain insensitive to the transcendent holiness of

God, His hatred of sin, and His uninfluenced mercy and grace offered to sinners through Jesus Christ, our Propitiation. For He was the One who "entered the Most Holy Place once for all, having obtained eternal redemption" (Heb. 9:12).

The enormous weight God places upon separation can also be seen in the Old Testament Sabbath, the sign of the Mosaic Covenant (Ex. 31:16) and the dominating feature of the Law. We read in Exodus 20:11 that God "blessed the Sabbath day and made it holy." The Sabbath day included numerous restrictions (Ex. 16:29, 23; 20:10; 35:1–3; Jer. 17:27; Neh. 10:31; Isa. 58:13–14) that forced the Jews to reflect upon their inability to keep the Law and admit that their only hope of salvation was in God's undeserved mercy and uninfluenced grace. There were eleven other Sabbaths God required, each designed to remind the people of His holiness, their sin, and their need for a Savior.

Along with the concept of separation, any definition of holiness must include the idea of *transcendence*, for indeed He is "the high and exalted One who lives forever, whose name is Holy, [who] dwell[s] on a high and holy place" (Isa. 57:15a). Holiness cannot be compared to anything we know, because all we know is unholy. Holiness is completely *other*, incomprehensible, and so unapproachable that even the seraphim who do His bidding cover their faces in His presence (Isa. 6:2). For the most part, holiness is undiscoverable apart from the illuminating work of the Spirit of God upon the heart where faith is present. It is therefore unspeakably transcendent. It is a mystery so vast, that apart from divine self-disclosure, it would remain forever unknown to us. And even with the help of the inspired Scriptures, we still find ourselves lost in wonder. Yet God commanded His covenant people, Israel, "Be holy; for I am holy" (Lev. 11:44). Also, speaking to His church, He said, "As obedient children, do not be conformed to the former lusts which were yours in your ignorance, but like the Holy One who called you, be holy yourselves also in all your behavior; because it is written, 'You shall be holy, for I am holy'" (1 Peter 1:14–16).

This indicates that *holiness primarily pertains to moral purity, being utterly separate from sin*. But a question naturally arises: "How can a person be holy when holiness is so obviously unattainable?"

The answer is found in the imputation of the righteousness of Christ, making the gospel itself unequalled in its power to transform sinners into saints. Because of sin, men and women stand before the bar of divine justice and hear the verdict—*guilty!*

Yet in the miracle of justification by faith, the sinless Savior stands in their place and assumes their guilt and bears their punishment. As a result, believers are not merely *treated as or even considered as righteous although they are still guilty.* No, this holy transaction is exceedingly more glorious. Instead, *sinners are declared to be actually righteous* (Rom. 3:21–24)—a gift far beyond pardon, even beyond forgiveness. Such a radical transformation shouts of God's hatred of sin and people's need for a righteousness that is not innately their own.

To be sure, *we are not holy.* We are sinful, in desperate need of a Savior—not a social redeemer. But because of the deceitfulness of heart, apart from regeneration, we will never see the horror of our sin and the glory of the cross. In fact, this is one of Satan's greatest strategies, for he as "the god of this world has blinded the minds of the unbelieving so that they might not see the light of the gospel of the glory of Christ" (2 Cor. 4:4). And there is perhaps no greater deception that has done more damage to the church than his distortion of what it means to be a Christian. It is therefore crucial that Christians understand the core doctrine of regeneration—a doctrine sure to arouse the ire of the unregenerate, and regrettably so.

The Miracle of Regeneration

God's ancient promise to spiritually regenerate His covenant people Israel was based upon a new and internalized covenant (Jer. 31:31–34) that would supersede the old covenant of the Mosaic law (2 Cor. 3:6) and was a promise extended to all who believe (2 Cor. 3:18). The assurance of a radical inward renovation that would transform Israel's moral and spiritual nature corresponds precisely with the New Testament promise of regeneration for all believers (John 3:3–8; Rom. 8:2, 5, 9; Gal. 5:22; Titus 3:5–7; 1 Peter 1:22).

The Greek term for "regeneration" (*palingenesia*) refers to *a supernatural, instantaneous impartation of spiritual life to the spiritually dead characterized by both washing and renewal.* Paul used the term in Titus 3:5–7: "He saved us, not on the basis of deeds which we have done in righteousness, but according to His mercy, by *the washing of regeneration and renewing by the Holy Spirit,* whom He poured out upon us richly through Jesus Christ our Savior, so that being justified by His grace we would be made heirs according to the hope of eternal life" (emphasis mine).

This is what Jesus referred to in John 3 when He told Nicodemus, the great teacher of Israel, "You must be born again" (v. 7); "Truly, Truly, I say to you, unless one is born again he cannot see the kingdom of God" (v. 3); and again in verse 5 Jesus said, "Truly, truly, I say to you, unless one is born of water and the Spirit he cannot *(oú dunatai)* enter into the kingdom of God." The use of *oú dunatai* translated "he cannot" underscores the fact that *man is utterly powerless to enter into the Kingdom of God by any other means whatsoever.*

Jesus' use of the phrase "born of water and the Spirit" taken from Ezekiel 36:24–27 (which has nothing to do with water baptism) would have resonated with Nicodemus who undoubtedly knew the passage well. He would have understood that the terms "water" and "Spirit" were frequently used together in the Old Testament to symbolize spiritual renewal and cleansing, the very things Nicodemus craved!

> For I will take you from the nations, gather you from all the lands and bring you into your own land. Then I will sprinkle clean water on you, and you will be clean; I will cleanse you from all your filthiness and from all your idols. Moreover, I will give you a new heart and put a new spirit within you; and I will remove the heart of stone from your flesh and give you a heart of flesh. I will put My Spirit within you and cause you to walk in My statutes, and you will be careful to observe My ordinances.
> (Ezek. 36:24–27)

Jesus didn't give this fastidious keeper of the law an additional list of religious duties to perform that would somehow enable him to cooperate with God's grace, because "it is the Spirit who gives life" (John 6:63). Man's soul is so corrupted by sin that nothing short of a total renovation can save him. All that man *is* and *does* is fundamentally offensive to our holy God, rendering him utterly unable to save himself. This is what makes the gospel such wonderfully good news! In regeneration, we are born "not of blood nor of the will of the flesh nor of the will of man, but of God" (John 1:13); man is entirely passive, wholly dependent upon the miraculous work of the Spirit. In light of this, we read in James 1:18: "In the exercise of His will He brought us forth by the word of truth."

Even as a child makes no contribution to his conception or birth in the physical realm—being totally dependent upon the activity of his parents—so, too, spiritually dead and depraved sinners make no contribution to their spiritual birth, being totally dependent upon the sovereign grace of God to raise them from spiritual death to life.

Regeneration Defined

I appreciate the definition of regeneration offered by a seventeenth-century Scottish pastor, David Dickson, who preached twenty-seven sermons on the subject in a town called Irvine, resulting in a mighty work of the Spirit in that realm. He defined regeneration this way:

> The natural man is incapable of seeing his need to be reconciled to God and wants nothing to do with it (1 Cor. 2:14). But with the miracle of the new birth, the sinner is given eyes to see his rebellion against God and ears to hear the truth of the gospel (Matt. 13:16–17). This is often called the effective (or efficacious) call of God, an operation of the Holy Spirit through the Word of God whereby individuals respond in faith and accept God's offer of salvation (Rom. 8:28–30; 1 Cor. 1:23–24; 2 Tim. 1:9; 1 Thess. 5:23–24; Eph. 1:18; 2 Peter 1:10). But the effective calling of God and regeneration seem to happen simultaneously, as Peter states, "For you have been born again not of seed which is perishable but

imperishable, that is, through the living and enduring word of God . . . and this is the word which was preached to you" (1 Peter 1:23, 25). Similarly, James says, "In the exercise of His will He brought us forth by the word of truth" (James 1:18). [49]

God's efficacious calling and regeneration results in the conviction of sin (Rom. 7:7), which in turn leads to repentant faith that *turns to Christ* for salvation and *turns away from sin and self-righteousness* (Acts 26:17–18; 1 Thess. 1:9). Because the natural man is dead in sin (Eph. 2:1–3) and thus unable to understand or accept the things of the Spirit of God (1 Cor. 2:14), repentant faith cannot occur apart from the new birth (John 1:13), a work in which sinners are entirely passive—for we "were born, not of blood nor of the will of the flesh nor of the will of man, but of God (John 1:13; *cf.* James 1:18; 1 Peter 1:3; John 3:3–8).

Without an awareness of the depths of our sin and the horror of the just punishment we deserve, salvation will never occur. Without an understanding of God's just wrath that abides upon deserving sinners (John 3:36), one cannot fully appreciate God's love for undeserving sinners. But with the miracle of regeneration, the Spirit quickens the dead to see both their sin and the atoning work of Christ for what they are, and thus renews the mind, heart, and will. Yet the vast majority of those who call themselves Christian today know nothing of this and therefore remain *unregenerate*. They have no awareness of their real need, resulting in a phony profession, a faith that cannot save, and an absence of spiritual discernment—topics we will now examine more closely.

Our Adversary the Devil

The primary source of deception is the *unseen enemy*, "[our] adversary the devil" (1 Peter 5:8), the father of lies (John 8:44), "the prince of the power of the air . . . the spirit that is now working in the sons of disobedience" (Eph. 2:2). The New Testament record is filled with warnings concerning the devil's implacable malice toward Christ and His church—a rage that gives rise to his in-

---

49   David Dickson, *Select Practical Writings of David Dickson*, Vol. 1 (Edinburgh: Printed for the Assemblies Committee, 1845), 211.

genious demonic deceptions that cause people to believe lies, "the mystery of lawlessness . . . already at work" in the world (2 Thess. 2:7; *cf.* Eph. 6:12). Paul's somber warning should grip us all: "But the Spirit explicitly says that in later times some will fall away from the faith, paying attention to deceitful spirits and doctrines of demons, by means of the hypocrisy of liars seared in their own conscience as with a branding iron" (2 Tim. 4:1–2).

Sadly, however, many professing evangelicals are indifferent to the existence of Satan and his strategies to destroy the true church in general, and their lives in particular. Few take seriously the warning to "put on the full armor of God, so that you will be able to stand firm against the schemes of the devil" (Eph. 6:11). The moral freefall and spiritual darkness in America is the inevitable consequence of unchecked human depravity and satanic blindness that have been able to thrive in a religious climate where the spiritual salt of evangelicalism has lost its savor and the light of the gospel has been all but extinguished by those who prefer darkness rather than light.

It was no mere coincidence that at the very birth of the church, the Spirit of God underscored the grave danger of satanic influence by revealing Satan's nefarious activities in two of its members. This chilling scene is recorded in Acts 5:3 when Peter said, "Ananias, why has Satan filled your heart to lie to the Holy Spirit?" The subsequent judgment against this man and his co-conspirator wife, Sapphira, caused "great fear [to come] upon the whole church, and upon all who heard of these things" (Acts 5:11).

But there is little fear in the church today. The sin of hypocrisy and the power of Satan to animate it within people who are superficially attached to the church (like Judas Iscariot) are seldom even seen, much less dealt with, in modern evangelicalism. Far too often, we hear a misguided cry for *ecclesiastical unity (ecumenism)*. But this can only be accomplished at the *expense of sound doctrine*—what Paul defined as "the unity of the faith, and of the knowledge of the Son of God" (Eph. 4:13). This has produced a mongrel church bereft of spiritual discernment and power. Much of modern evangelicalism has become nothing more than an amorphous entity controlled by the prevailing winds of culture rather than by the Word of God.

Over the course of my lifetime, I have witnessed a frightening "openness" mentality that has now evolved into a full-blown ecumenical ethos that cannot coexist with the New Testament church whose spiritual authenticity can be seen most clearly in the Protestant church of the Reformation. "People of faith," as religious people are often called, prefer *conversations* to *proclamations*—despite God's mandate to the contrary (Matt. 28:19–20; 1 Tim. 4:13; 2 Tim. 2:2; 4:2; Titus 2:1). Avant-garde evangelicals consider biblical preaching to be passé, authoritarian, and sectarian. They prefer motivational speeches, conversational sermonettes, and dialogues between various faith communities—modes of communication that value *experience* over *truth* and tolerance of all views (except biblical Christianity), no matter how absurd or contradictory. Because of this, any attempt to "contend earnestly for the faith" (Jude 3) is considered to be an unacceptable act of arrogance and intolerance, contrary to the humility and love of Christ.

The command to "examine everything carefully; hold fast to that which is good; abstain from every form of evil" (1 Thess. 5:20–22) has therefore fallen on deaf ears. Because few pastors today are willing to confront and attack error (2 Cor. 10:3–5), most churches are not "the household of God . . . the pillar and support of the truth" (1 Tim. 3:15). Instead, they have become the dwelling place of Satan . . . the pillar and support of deception. Iain Murray refutes this modern "openness" writing:

> Instead of believers in the apostolic age being directed to listen to all views "with an open mind", they were told how to "test the spirits, whether they are of God" (1 John 4:1). For there are "deceiving spirits and doctrines of demons" (1 Tim. 4:1); false teachers "who will secretly bring in destructive heresies" (2 Peter 2:1). There are words which "spread as a cancer" (2 Tim. 2:17).[50]

While many professing evangelicals will reject extreme doctrinal perversions and wholly affirm (at least in principle) the doctrinal truths of historic Protestant orthodoxy, many do,

50 Iain H. Murray, *Evangelicalism Divided: A Record of Crucial Change in the Years 1950 to 2000* (Edinburgh: The Banner of Truth Trust, 2000), 69.

however, embrace the values and priorities of contemporary culture so strongly that they cannot be distinguished from the world—perhaps the most ingenious of all Satan's strategies to deceive.

As a result, countless numbers of people have responded to a watered-down gospel carefully crafted to attract virtually anyone regardless of what he or she believes about the glory of the Person and work of the Lord Jesus Christ. Churches are then populated with unbelievers who "did not receive the love of the truth so as to be saved" (2 Thess. 2:10); who "[do] not accept the things of the Spirit of God" and "cannot understand them, because they are spiritually appraised" (1 Cor. 2:14). This was at the heart of the apostle Paul's great concern for the church at Corinth when the people there were being taught a different gospel, causing him to say, "But I am afraid, lest as the serpent deceived Eve by his craftiness, your minds should be led astray from the simplicity and purity of devotion to Christ" (2 Cor. 11:3). Would that all churches share such a concern.

With churches filled with people who are "Christian" in name only, it is little wonder that "they will not endure sound doctrine . . . and will turn away their ears from the truth, and will turn aside to myths" (2 Tim. 4:3–4). Bottom line, much of the church today is made up of unbelievers. This is why we witness such an abysmal lack of discernment in ostensibly evangelical churches that are content to live in a fool's paradise of satanic deception. It is frightening to witness churches that are "open" to the false doctrines of Roman Catholicism and the Word of Faith cult, or actually promote unbiblical ideologies like the LGBTQ agenda, radical feminism, and progressive liberal (often Marxist) politics. And what is most telling is that even the gentlest rebuke is met with hostility so fierce that it can only be accurately described as demonic.

The Inevitable Consequence of Worldliness

As Satan sows tares among the wheat, much of evangelicalism has taken on a whole new image. Its obsession with church growth at the expense of sound doctrine has shifted the church's purpose as the proclaimer and protector of divine truth (1 Tim. 3:15; Titus 2:1, 15) into an amorphous amalgam of social services, pseudo-Christian entertainment, prosperity hustling, and political activism. Worse yet, rather than heeding the command to come out and be separate from the world (2 Cor. 6:14–18), the church has become more like the world, a phenomenon that produces success in the eyes of man, but triggers judgment in the eyes of God. Iain Murray describes this dynamic:

> . . . evangelicals, while commonly retaining the same set of beliefs, have been tempted to seek success in ways which the New Testament identifies as "worldliness". Worldliness is departing from God. It is a man-centered way of thinking; it proposes objectives which demand no radical breach with man's fallen nature; it judges the importance of things by the present and material results; it weighs success by numbers; it covets human esteem and wants no unpopularity; it knows no truth for which it is worth suffering; it declines to be a "fool for Christ's sake". Worldliness is the mind-set of the unregenerate. It adopts idols and is at war with God. . . . It is professing Christians who are asked, "Do you not know that the friendship of the world is enmity with God?" (James 4:4) and are commanded, "Do not love the world", "keep yourselves from idols" (1 John 2:15, 5:21).[51]

Apostasy generally arises in the church just because this danger ceases to be observed.

The consequence is that spiritual warfare gives way to spiritual pacifism, and, in the same spirit, the church devises ways to present the gospel which will neutralize any offense. The antithesis between regenerate and unregenerate is passed over and it is supposed that the interests and ambitions of the unconverted can somehow be harnessed to win their approval for Christ. Then when this approach achieves "results"—as it will—no more justification is thought to be needed. The rule of Scripture has given place to pragmatism. The apostolic statement, "For if I still please men, I would not be the servant of Christ" (Gal. 1:10), has lost its meaning.

---

51   Ibid., 254–55.

Evidence of the New Birth

When, through the power of the revealed Word of God, the Spirit moves upon a sinner's heart and causes him to be "born again" (John 3:3, 7), the supernatural gift of faith is suddenly imparted. Spiritually blinded eyes can suddenly see the light of Christ's glory (2 Cor. 4:4–6; *cf.* John 3:3; Heb. 11:1), making the sinner's perception of light (regeneration) the *cause*, not the *effect* of faith. For indeed, spiritual cadavers in a state of spiritual death (Eph. 2:1–3) whose minds are "hostile toward God and cannot subject [themselves] to the law of God" (Rom. 8:7) are utterly incapable of understanding the things of the Spirit, much less embracing them in repentant faith (1 Cor. 2:14). In 1 John 5:4, the apostle writes, "For everyone who has been born of God overcomes the world. And this is the victory that has overcome the world—our faith." Similarly, Jesus told Nicodemus, "Unless one is born again he cannot see the kingdom of God" (John 3:3)—the utopia the world seeks in futility.

With the new birth, Christ is miraculously formed in the heart (Gal. 4:2) and the newborn saint is "renewed to a true knowledge according to the image of the One who created him" (Col. 3:10)— just as God had predestined in eternity past (Rom. 8:29). Sinners become saints and are suddenly made partakers of the divine nature (2 Peter 1:4), causing them to bear a resemblance to the image of God.

The Spirit-wrought transformation in the soul causes a man to see the dreadful condition of his sinful heart and the undeserved mercy, grace, and love of Christ that he now embraces in saving faith. Though we "formerly lived in the lusts of our flesh, indulging the desires of the flesh and of the mind, and were by nature children of wrath" the Spirit "made us alive together with Christ" (Eph. 2:3, 5). At the moment of our new birth, we are made new creatures in Christ, setting into motion a process of sanctification what will culminate in Christlikeness, for "that which is born of the flesh is flesh, and what which is born of the Spirit is spirit" (John 3:6; John 1:13; 1 Peter 1:23). The life of the newborn saint is characterized by overcoming the wicked influences of Satan's world system (1 John 5:4)—including a newfound hatred for what he or she once loved, and a love for what he or she once hated. The Spirit plants within us new desires, loves, passions, inclinations, beliefs, and values (2 Cor. 5:17) so that we manifest the fruit of the Spirit: "love, joy, peace, patience, kindness, goodness, faithfulness, gentleness, self-control" (Gal. 5:22–23).

With the disposition of the soul radically changed, God's desires become our desires (Ps. 37:4) and He causes us "to become obedient from the heart to that form of teaching to which [we] were committed" (Rom. 6:17; cf. 1 John 2:23–24), for indeed, "If you know that He is righteous, you know that everyone also who practices righteousness is born of Him" (1 John 2:29).

Having been delivered from the power of sin and the penalty of the law, "the requirement of the law is fulfilled in us," according to Romans 8:4, "who do not walk according to the flesh, but according to the Spirit, though the body is dead because of sin, yet our spirit is alive because of His righteousness." And as the newly implanted seed of divine life begins to germinate and bear fruit, the Spirit uses the Word of God to grow us into the likeness of Christ (1 Peter 1:23), causing us to constantly be putting to death the principle of sin that remains incarcerated in our unredeemed humanness (Rom. 7:14–25) through the habitual and joyful putting away of reoccurring manifestations of sin and putting on patterns of righteousness (Eph. 4:22–24).

Evidence of regeneration will also include an intimate love for Christ that animates a personal pursuit of holiness that includes a longing for personal fellowship with Him through prayer and worship (John 15:4, 7), a love for other believers (1 John 3:14), and a subjective awareness of the love of God and the Spirit's leading in our life in obedience to the will of God (Rom. 8:15–16; cf. 1 John 4:13).

As every twice-born saint will attest, the miracle of spiritual sight wrought within the soul by the power of the Holy Spirit will set into motion the most soul-satisfying and soul-exhilarating realities known to man, but not to any man, for this is only available to those who, by the regenerating power of sovereign grace, place their trust in the Lord Jesus Christ as the only hope of their salvation. Only then will our adversary be defeated.

6

. . . .

The Christian's Assurance

Trusting in God's Sovereign Rule and Purposes

I am the Lord, there is no other. Besides Me there is no God...
The One forming light and creating darkness, causing well-
being and creating calamity;
I am the Lord who does all these.

Isaiah 45:6–7

I received a text early one morning from a young pastor friend I have had the joy of mentoring who asked me to call him at my convenience, which I did. After getting caught up on each other's life and ministry, he said (and this is close paraphrase), "Well brother, I need some help. I know they're still counting votes, but it looks like Biden and the godless socialists have won the election and my people are really struggling. *I'm really struggling!* We know how corrupt and evil these people are. We know we can't trust the vote count, can't trust the media, can't trust the government. And we know what Romans 13 says about being in subjection to government authorities that God has placed over us. But we also know how these people hate true Christians. So this is really scary. And yes, we know God is sovereign and He has allowed this to happen, but we're all frustrated and afraid. I'm just not real sure I know what to tell them. So what are you telling your folks?"

What is truly remarkable is that over the course of the next few days I heard from three other pastors and many other believers who shared the same concerns. They all expressed how an evil darkness has consumed our country over the past year or so, like the smoke of a massive forest fire enveloping a city with choking fumes. While many will laugh and call this the hyperbole of religious fanatics, those of us who know and love Christ are all too aware of what is really happening. Between the truths of Scripture and the illuminating work of the indwelling Spirit of God, we are able to discern what the rest of the world cannot see (1 Cor. 2:14–16; *cf.* Heb. 5:14). This chapter is basically a summary of my answer to the young pastor in my illustration and the essence of what I have shared with many others.

We Will Not Bow

To be sure, these are frightening times. While many of the policies of the Republicans are blatantly unbiblical, those of the Democrats take evil to a whole new level. Their neo-Marxist agenda combined with moral policies that are considered abominations in the eyes of God are satanic to the core. Secular extremists and anti-religious forces already in federal, state, and local governments will use them (as they have already) to threaten our religious freedom (along with other protected rights in the Constitution). Just their commitment to pass the Equality Act (discussed in chapter 2) reveals their disdain for biblical Christians—an animosity that is eclipsed only by their utter contempt for Christ. Even non-Christians are fleeing liberal cities and states to escape polices they describe as draconian and insane, and what Scripture describes as satanic (Eph. 2:2) and depraved (Rom. 1:18)—evidence of the wrath of divine abandonment.

I personally know many Christians who have lost their businesses and even their jobs because they refused to bow to the god of political correctness. To be sure, faithful believers simply will not submit to the gods of culture that Satan has erected. They will not attend mandated "Diversity" and "Sensitivity" workshops to have Critical Race Theory, Radical Feminism, and LGBTQ perversions crammed down their throat. They will not participate in the BLM protests, Gay Pride parades, or "Celebrate Diversity" festivities. They will not allow their children to be indoctrinated by leftist elites in public schools who embrace the neo-Marxist, social justice, and LGBTQ agendas. They will not comply with government officials who exceed their legitimate jurisdiction and impose unnecessary restrictions on church services based upon exaggerated and politically motivated public health fears due to the COVID outbreak.

Because of our love for the One who first loved us, we will not serve the gods of culture and neither will we bow to the golden image of secular humanism. To government officials, we respectfully say with the apostles, "Whether it is right in the sight of God to give heed to you rather than to God, you be the judge" (Acts 4:19). And our unreserved reply to that question is the same as the apostles gave: "We must obey God rather than men" (Acts 5:29). We fear God, not man. No matter how many hate-crime laws are passed to harass, intimidate, silence, and jail us because we dare to disagree with the societal norms of politically correct orthodoxy, we will only obey the One true and living God. Despite the threats, our response will be like that of Shadrach, Meshach, and Abed-nego to Nebuchadnezzar when he threatened to burn them alive for refusing to worship the golden image of himself that he had erected:

If it be so, our God whom we serve is able to deliver us from the furnace of blazing fire; and He will deliver us out of your hand, O king. But even if He does not, let it be known to you, O king, that we are not going to serve your gods or worship the golden image that you have set up.
(Dan. 3:17–18)

Historically, the two main persecutors of the church have always been secular government and false religion. So what we see in America today is nothing new. "Indeed," Scripture says, "all who desire to live godly in Christ Jesus will be persecuted" (2 Tim. 3:12). After being stoned and left for dead, Paul strengthened and encouraged the disciples to continue in the faith saying, "Through many tribulations we must enter the kingdom of God" (Acts 14:19–22). Likewise, Christ promised: "If they persecuted Me, they will also persecute you" (John 15:20). In the last of the beatitudes, He said, "Blessed are you when people insult you and persecute you, and falsely say all kinds of evil against you because of Me. Rejoice and be glad, for your reward in heaven is great; for in the same way they persecuted the prophets who were before you" (Matt. 5:11–12).

Evangelism, Edification, and Encouragement

My purpose is not to inflame hatred toward those who hate us. They're our mission field. They're people alienated from God, darkened in their understanding, and in desperate need of the gospel. They need our *compassion*, not our *contempt*. Indeed, Jesus has commanded us "to love [our] enemies and pray for those who persecute [us]" (Matt. 5:44). They need a change of heart that only Christ can produce, and we must be committed to that end for His sake, remembering that were it not for saving grace, our scoffing voices would be heard among them. Bottom line: *Americans who detest us need us to love them enough to give them the gospel in the fullness of its purity and power; so let us pray that they might believe unto salvation.*

My purpose here is to edify and encourage true Christians, undoubtedly the vast majority of the people reading this book.

My intention is summed in Paul's admonition to Timothy:

> I solemnly charge you in the presence of God and of Christ Jesus, who is to judge the living and the dead, and by His appearing and His kingdom: preach the word; be ready in season and out of season; reprove, rebuke, exhort, with great patience and instruction. For the time will come when they will not endure sound doctrine; but wanting to have their ears tickled, they will accumulate for themselves teachers in accordance to their own desires, and will turn away their ears from the truth and will turn aside to myths. But you, be sober in all things, endure hardship, do the work of an evangelist, fulfill your ministry.
> (2 Tim. 4:1–5)

Consistent with these admonitions, we must turn to the Word of God for answers to how we as Christians should respond to the mounting hostility the true church is experiencing during these dark days. Two extremes seem to currently exist: *activism* and *apathy*. Both are unbiblical. While there are many God-honoring responses found in Scripture, I wish to share a few that are representative of the advice I gave the young pastor as well as many other believers whom I've had the joy of interacting with, including my own congregation. Now is not a time for wringing our hands in desperation or despair. It is not a time for political and social activism, and it is certainly not a time to yield to apathy and say, "Well, there's nothing I can do anyway, so who cares. Let God handle it." Now is a time to say, "Lord, these are frightening times, but I trust You completely. I know You are up to great things to bring glory to Yourself, so please show me what You would have me do to that end."

FIRST, *we must see these evil days as an opportunity to trust in God's sovereign rule and purposes to ultimately bring glory to Himself.*

In times of fear and uncertainty, we must never lose sight of God's sovereignty—*His absolute rule and authority over all things.* Like perhaps no other doctrine, this is the greatest source of comfort to the redeemed when experiencing some profound adversity or loss in life. Knowing God is fully *aware of* and *in charge of* all that happens instantly delegitimizes thoughts of abandonment, indifference, or randomness (though in our humanness, we are bound to *feel* otherwise). Nothing catches Him by surprise, including when His people are persecuted. Indeed, He is a *sovereign*, not a *contingent,* God. There is therefore nothing in our life He has not *ordained to accomplish, allow,* or *understand completely*, including the sufferings, tragedies, and atrocities we experience. His character is in no need of *rescue*, nor is it even remotely worthy of *attack.*

Trusting in God's Sovereignty

Regarding His *sovereignty*, we must remember that he is the One who, "[declares] the end from the beginning, and from ancient times things which have not been done, saying, 'My purpose will be established, and I will accomplish all My good pleasure'" (Isa. 46:10). There is nothing man can do to escape His influence: "The mind of man plans his way, but the Lord directs his steps" (Prov. 16:9; *cf.* Jer. 10:23). Daniel says, "He removes kings and establishes kings" (2:21), and he described God as the One who "does according to His will in the host of heaven and among the inhabitants of earth; and no one can ward off His hand or say to Him, 'What have You done?'" (4:35; *cf.* Ps. 135:6). In these and many other verses, God leaves no doubt that He reigns in absolute sovereignty over His creation as the One who "works all things after the counsel of His will" (Eph. 1:11). This also speaks to the *immensity* of God (that He fills all space and transcends it) and the *omnipresence* of God (that His entire being is present with every point of space)—subjects beyond the scope of this discussion, but inextricably bound to it (see Gen. 14:19, 22; Deut. 10:14; 1 Kings 8:27; 2 Chron. 2:6; Isa. 66:1; Ps. 139:7-10; Jer. 23:23-24; Acts 7:48-49; 17:27-28; Col. 1:16; Rev. 10:6).

What a comforting truth to know that no matter how bad our circumstances, how hopeless our condition, how unfair our plight, God is ultimately in absolute rule and authority over all things, and His purposes for our eternal welfare and His ineffable majesty cannot be thwarted.

Trusting in God's Omniscience

Regarding His *omniscience*, we can also find comfort knowing, "The LORD looks from heaven; He sees all the sons of men; from His dwelling place He looks out on all the inhabitants of the earth, He who fashions the hearts of them all, He who understands all their works" (Ps. 33:13–15). He's perfectly and intimately aware of all that is happening in our country, even the thoughts of the wicked. His knowledge is infinitely perfect and requires no further information (Isa. 40:13–14; Rom. 11:34); it precedes all things outside of Himself and is never obtained from anything that exists outside Himself (Rom. 8:29; 1 Cor. 2:7; Eph. 1:4–5; 2 Tim. 1:9). For this reason, in utter awe David described how God knew the minutest details of his life (Ps. 139:1–6). In Psalm 147, the Lord is praised as the One who heals the brokenhearted; the One who "counts the number of the stars; He gives names to all of them. Great is our Lord and abundant in strength; His understanding is infinite" (v. 5).

There is nothing man can think or do that escapes His notice, and this includes *tragedies* and *atrocities* that take place, "For the ways of a man are before the eyes of the LORD, and He watches all his paths" (Prov. 5:21). Indeed, "The eyes of the LORD are in every place, watching the evil and the good" (Prov. 15:3). "His understanding is inscrutable" (Isa. 40:28); "There is no creature hidden from His sight, but all things are open and laid bare to the eyes of Him with whom we have to do" (Heb. 4:13); "He knows everything" (1 John 3:19).

While this fallen world is plagued by every imaginable form of evil and "the sufferings of Christ are ours in abundance" (2 Cor. 1:5), we can find relief knowing His sanctifying purposes are always at work in our lives and nothing happens outside the sphere of His ultimate control and intimate awareness. For this reason, Paul exhorts us to "exult in our tribulations" (Rom. 5:3)— not merely rejoice in spite of them or resign ourselves to them and somehow choose to be happy; not even rejoice in the midst of them, though that is important. What he is saying is that we are to exult *because* of our tribulations, *on account* of them! And he goes on to tell us why: "Knowing that tribulation brings about perseverance; and perseverance, proven character; and proven character, hope; and hope does not disappoint, because the love of God has been poured out within our hearts through the Holy Spirit who was given to us" (Rom. 5:3–5). He obviously understood that God ordains and oversees our afflictions for our good and His glory, though we seldom see it at the time.

To be sure, it requires a special measure of Spirit-empowered faith to trust God in the fires of affliction, knowing that all that is burned off is our dross. But only then can we have the confidence to say with Job, "When He has tried me, I shall come forth as gold" (Job 23:10). No saint will be able to survive the great sorrows of life unless he or she understands and fully rejoices in the weighty truth that *authentic faith must and will be tested by fire* (1 Peter 1:7). An untested faith is a dubious faith, and an untried commitment is an unreliable commitment. Therefore, through His *sovereignty* and *omniscience,* He accomplishes His glorious purposes in the lives of those He loves, conforming us into the likeness of Christ.

With confidence we can therefore join the psalmist and declare, "The judgments of the LORD are true; they are righteous altogether" (Ps. 19:19)—even when He has ordained to allow disaster to befall us. Speaking through Isaiah, the Lord said, "I am the LORD, there is no other. Besides Me there is no God . . . . The One forming light and creating darkness, causing well-being and creating calamity; I am the LORD who does all these" (Isa. 45:6–7). Likewise, the prophet Jeremiah lamented, "Is it not from the mouth of the Most High that both good and ill go forth?" (Lam. 3:38).

Solomon reminds us that, "the LORD has made all things for Himself, even the wicked for the day of evil" (see Prov. 16:4). Hannah praised God's sovereignty—even over evil—when she prayed, "The LORD puts to death and makes alive; He brings down to Sheol and brings up. The LORD makes poor and rich; He humbles, He also exalts." (1 Sam. 2:6–7). The prophet Amos also declared, "If a disaster occurs in a city, has the LORD not brought it about?" (Amos 3:6).

We never know for sure what God may be up to when suffering as a result of evil afflicts us in some painful and unexpected way. We can never know God's secret will (Deut. 29:29); we can only submit to it, confident that it comes from the hand of a loving Father. We have trials because we need them, and we have no more of them than we need.

I'm sure Joseph felt confused when his brothers captured him and sold him into slavery—a great example of God's providence orchestrating evil through the choices of sinful individuals. The essence of this doctrinal truth can be seen when Joseph forgave the sinful acts of his brothers and said, "As for you, you meant evil against me, but God meant it for good in order to bring about this present result, to preserve many people alive" (Gen. 50:20).

Lessons from the Trials of Job

Trusting God, come what may, is at the very heart of the Christian faith. But it goes against our nature, especially when we experience evil, whether it's physical or moral.

The account of Job portrays this struggle. In that fascinating historical account revealed to us by inspiration of the Spirit of God through His author (perhaps Moses or Solomon), Satan refutes God's claims of Job's righteousness, insisting Job's faith and obedience were merely a manipulative ploy to gain divine blessings. But God knew otherwise. He knew that Job's righteousness was not that of his own, but a supernatural gift of God given to bring glory to Himself. Knowing how he had seduced the holy angels to join his original rebellion (*cf.* Isa. 14:12ff.; Ezek. 28:11ff.; Rev. 12:4), Satan probably assumed he would have no problem doing the same with Job—or any other person who trusted God. No doubt he believed that if he could inflict enough suffering and pain, Job would "curse God and die!" (Job 2:9)—as his wife later counseled him to do.

So with the purpose of proving Satan wrong and thereby proving the unfailing power of genuine saving faith, He consented to allow Satan to test Job. While Job's faith never failed (see 13:15), it did falter under the weight of unexplained, undeserved, and unbearable suffering and loss. As the pain and sorrow increased, Job repeatedly called God to court in order to verify his innocence.

But what is truly fascinating is that never once did God give Job an audience to present his case. Never once did God even explain how He had squared off with Satan to prove how saving faith cannot be destroyed, no matter how severe the trials, and how he (Job) was the test case to forever substantiate His divine assertion. Never once did God allow Himself to be dragged into court by His sinful creatures. Instead, He responded to Job's demand for a judicial hearing by intimidating him with His glory! He began by saying,

> Then the LORD answered Job out of the whirlwind and said,
> "Who is this that darkens counsel
> By words without knowledge?
> "Now gird up your loins like a man,
> And I will ask you, and you instruct Me!
> "Where were you when I laid the foundation of the earth?
> Tell Me, if you have understanding,
> Who set its measurements? Since you know.
> Or who stretched the line on it?
> "On what were its bases sunk?
> Or who laid its cornerstone,
> When the morning stars sang together
> And all the sons of God shouted for joy?"
> (Job 38:1–7)

The sheer force of God's intimidation and humiliation put Job in his place (as it does all of us). Job was forced to face the reality that no matter how severe and inexplicably unfair the trial, *God is never to be challenged. He is only to be trusted.* For He alone is the Creator, Sustainer, Controller, Redeemer, and Consummator of all things. Job learned that to even question such a transcendent, omniscient, omnipotent God was the height of folly, and he became deeply convicted that to be so presumptuous as to even insinuate that God is unfair was an act of high treason against the Most High.

Then, as expected, Job humbled himself before God, even though he had lost everything except his life, and he said this:

> "I know that You can do all things,
> And that no purpose of Yours can be thwarted.

'Who is this that hides counsel without knowledge?"
"Therefore I have declared that which I did not understand,
Things too wonderful for me, which I did not know."
'Hear, now, and I will speak;
I will ask You, and You instruct me.'
"I have heard of You by the hearing of the ear;
But now my eye sees You;
Therefore I retract,
And I repent in dust and ashes ."
(Job 42:2–6)

Though his circumstances had not changed, his perspective had changed drastically. His presumptuous pride and ignorance gave way to humility and wisdom. All the answers he and his friends concocted to explain God's reasons for inflicting so much suffering on him were worthless and mistaken, worthy only of God's rebuke (42:7). In fact, God never gave him an explanation—not only because He didn't owe him one, but also because Job couldn't understand it if He did. Why the innocent suffer is an inscrutable mystery known only to God who has ordained it for purposes that ultimately contribute to His glory—a lesson we all must learn. The tragic consequences of living in a fallen, sin-cursed world are inevitable, albeit more severe for some than others—a reality that should cause every believer to hate sin all the more and rejoice in the certain hope that we will one day be delivered from every appearance and effect of evil.

Then, as if to demonstrate His unfailing love and compassion, God restored Job's health, fortunes, and family; when he prayed for his friends, "the LORD increased all that he had twofold" (42:10). James' commentary on Job's ordeal underscores God's compassion and mercy when he says, "We count those blessed who endured. You have heard of the endurance of Job and have seen the outcome of the Lord's dealings, that the Lord is full of compassion and is merciful" (James 5:11).

God Is Worthy To Be Trusted

From this amazing real-life illustration that God has graciously given to us, we can see most vividly that *God has a right to be trusted,* and *He is worthy to be trusted.* And can there be any greater comfort than knowing we will one day bask in the fullness of His goodness for eternity? I think not. The perfections of His attributes and the magnitude of His sovereign power are exceedingly beyond anything we can possibly comprehend. His ineffable glory and eternal grace humble us to the core. We must therefore bow our heads in breathless adoration and acknowledge that we, as creatures, have no right to question our Creator. He has the right to do as He pleases. Because of this, when we find ourselves in some crucible of grace, we must never ask, "Why?" We must only ask, "What?" "What can I do to demonstrate my unfailing trust in You, my God?" Then with Moses we should relax and say, "The secret things belong to the LORD" (Deut. 29:29). We must say, "I cannot possibly understand Your plans and purposes, nor could I comprehend them if You were to explain them. So I will curse sin and I will praise You for every expression of Your goodness even in my sorrow and pain, casting all my anxiety on You, because You care for me" (1 Peter 5:7).

By considering the manifestation of these great truths in the life of Job, and many other characters in Scripture, we are humbled by the following truths that should permeate our heart, especially in days of trouble:

- There are matters going on in heaven with God that believers know nothing about; yet, they affect their lives;
- Even the best effort at explaining the issues of life can be useless;
- God's people do suffer. Bad things happen all the time to good people, so one cannot judge a person's spirituality by his painful circumstances or successes;
- Even though God seems far away, perseverance in faith is a most noble virtue since God is good and one can safely leave one's life in His hands;
- The believer in the midst of suffering should not abandon

God, but draw near to Him, so out of the fellowship can come the comfort—even without the explanation;

• Suffering may be intense, but it will ultimately end for the righteous and God will bless abundantly.[52]

How Long, O Lord?

Those who truly love God can find some measure of comfort even when their emotional knees buckle under the crushing weight of suffering, knowing that "God causes all things to work together for good to those who love God, to those who are called according to His purpose" (Rom. 8:28). But none of us is immune to soul-crushing despair. Even our Savior needed an angel from heaven to strengthen Him. "And being in agony He was praying very fervently; and His sweat became like drops of blood, falling down upon the ground" (Luke 22:44). So *when*, not *if*, we find ourselves despairing of life itself, feeling as though God has abandoned us in our pain and we are left to our own resources, there is no shame in crying aloud with the psalmist, "How long, O LORD? Will You forget me forever? How long will You hide Your face from me?" (Psalm 13:1). But even then, when all seems lost, our confidence must remain in the goodness and faithfulness of God who is still at work and who will eventually deliver us from our affliction. Knowing this, the psalmist followed up his plaintiff lament and said, "But I have trusted in Your lovingkindness; My heart shall rejoice in Your salvation. I will sing to the LORD, Because He has dealt bountifully with me" (vv. 5–6).

SECOND, *we must see these evil days as an opportunity to relax in the agencies of God's providence to orchestrate all things for our good and His glory.*

As I reflect upon the countless times as a pastor that I have had the privilege of comforting those in great distress, and when I consider the multiple sorrows I have experienced personally, I realize that these great truths regarding God's perfections and sovereign purposes are always the Spirit-empowered remedy for

---

52   *The MacArthur Study Bible* (Nashville, Tennessee: Thomas Nelson, 1997), 694.

every sickness of the soul and every loss of the heart. Emboldened and encouraged by them, my faith is fortified, and I can honestly say that when the night is the darkest, God's presence is the brightest. This was David's testimony when surrounded by great terror he testified,

> But as for me, I trust in You, O LORD, I say, "You are my God." My times are in Your hand; Deliver me from the hand of my enemies, and from those who persecute me, Make Your face to shine upon Your servant; Save me in Your lovingkindness. . . How great is Your goodness, which You have stored up for those who fear You, which You have wrought for those who take refuge in You.
> (Psalm 31:14–16, 19)

To know that God is always up to something in our life is utterly incomprehensible. But He is. Even when life hurts and we don't want to go on. And in those times of hopelessness and helplessness, the rich truths that emerge from Paul's familiar words in Romans 8:28 take on new meaning: "And we know that God causes all things to work together for good to those who love God, to those who are called according to His purpose." Knowing that in His sweet providence He is orchestrating every temptation, every sorrow, even every sin, to accomplish His purposes in our life both now and for eternity is a reality that should cause our troubled soul to find peace even in the greatest tempest.

The wise and godly Puritan, Thomas Watson, unpacks this great text in ways that I have personally found most helpful in his book, *All Things for Good*. Here is a sample for your benefit. He states,

> If all things work for good, hence learn that there is a providence. Things do not work of themselves, but God sets them working for good. God is the great Disposer of all events and issues. He sets everything working. "His kingdom ruleth over all" (Psalm 103.19). It is meant of His providential kingdom. Things in the world are not governed by second causes, by the counsels of men, by the stars and planets, but by

divine providence. Providence is the queen and governess of the world. There are three things in providence: God's foreknowing, God's determining, and God's directing all things to their periods and events. Whatever things do work in the world, God sets them a working.[53]

He goes on to offer moving reminders of the many ways we can witness the providences of God at work in our lives, perhaps unwittingly; evoking within us the breathless adoration He deserves. He says,

See here the wisdom of God, who can make the worst things imaginable turn to the good of the saints. He can by a divine chemistry extract gold out of dross. "Oh the depth of the wisdom of God!" (Rom. 11:33). It is God's great design to set forth the wonder of His wisdom. The Lord made Joseph's prison a step to preferment. There was no way for Jonah to be saved, but by being swallowed up. God suffered the Egyptians to hate Israel (Psalm 106:41), and this was the means of their deliverance. The apostle Paul was bound with a chain, and that chain which did bind him was the means of enlarging the gospel (Phil. 1:12). God enriches by impoverishing; He causes the augmentation of grace by the diminution of an estate. When the creature goes further from us, it is that Christ may come nearer to us. God works strangely. He brings order out of confusion, harmony out of discord. He frequently makes use of unjust men to do that which is just. "He is wise in heart" (Job 9:4). He can reap His glory out of men's fury (Ps. 76:10). Either the wicked shall not do the hurt that they intend, or they shall do the good which they do not intend. God often helps when there is least hope, and saves His people in that way which they think will destroy. He made use of the high-priest's malice and Judas' treason to redeem the world. Through indiscreet passion, we are apt to find fault with things that happen; which is as if an illiterate man should censure philosophy, or a blind man find fault with the work in a landscape. "Vain man would be wise" (Job 11:12). Silly animals will be taxing

---

53 Thomas Watson, *All Things For Good* (1663; reprint, Carlisle, Pennsylvania: The Banner of Truth Trust, 2001), 55–56.

Providence, and calling the wisdom of God to the bar of reason. God's ways are "past finding out" (Rom. 11:33). They are rather to be admired than fathomed. There is never a providence of God, but has either a mercy or a wonder in it. How stupendous and infinite is that wisdom, that makes the most adverse dispensations work for the good of His children![54]

THIRD, *we must remember that even in these evil days, Christ is building His church as promised.*

No one likes cheaters, except other cheaters who benefit from it. It's okay to look the other way when their team bends the rules a bit to gain the victory, or when their political party pulls some shenanigans to win an election, or when their lawyer trumps up some phony charges to win their case. But oh, when the shoe is on the other foot, they cry, "Unfair!"

As Christians, we're used to being cheated. Satan and his entire world system are against us. It is like playing football where the other team gets eight downs to our four, double the points, and the refs are on their payroll. It can be really discouraging. We're the target of cancel culture, the punch line of politically correct jokes, and the forbidden voice in public discourse. Virtually all the values of orthodox evangelicalism are being systematically outlawed. But as in the account of Joseph and his brothers who betrayed him, what Satan means for evil, God means for good. Persecution always purges the church.

Evidence of God Purging and Purifying His Church

Every metric shows a steady decrease in practicing Christians, which proves they were Christian in name only. "They went out from us, but they were not really of us; for if they had been of us, they would have remained with us; but they went out, so that it would be shown that they all are not of us" (1 John 2:19). Here are some statistics according to Barna Group research on the state of the church:

---

54   Ibid., 60–61.

In 2000, 45 percent of all those sampled qualified as practicing Christians. That share has consistently declined over
the last 19 years. Now, just one in four Americans (25%) is
a practicing Christian. In essence, the share of practicing
Christians has nearly dropped in half since 2000. Where did
these practicing Christians go? The data indicate that their
shift was evenly split. Half of them fell away from consistent faith engagement, essentially becoming non-practicing
Christians (2000: 35% vs. 2020: 43%), while the other half
moved into the non-Christian segment (2000: 20% vs. 2019:
30%). This shift also contributed to the growth of the atheist
/ agnostic / none segment, which has nearly doubled in size
during this same amount of time (2003: 11% vs. 2018: 21%).[55]

Between these trends and the hostility of a pagan American
culture, one might think the Christian church will soon find itself
in the trash heap of obsolete religious superstitions that no longer
have any relevance. Already America mirrors the dark paganism
of Europe. According to the *American Worldview Inventory
2020*, religious syncretism is becoming the dominant religious
worldview.

Popular beliefs include:

- there is no absolute moral truth (58%);
- basis of truth are factors or sources other than God (58%);
- right and wrong is determined by factors other than the
  Bible (77%);
- the Bible is not the authoritative and true word of God (59%);
- people are basically good (69%);
- and the personal definition of success is not based on consistent obedience to God (79%).[56]

Dr. George Barna, CRC Director of Research and author of
the *American Worldview Inventory 2020,* called this latest survey
discouraging but consistent with prior findings.

---

55 https://www.barna.com/research/changing-state-of-the-church/
56 https://www.arizonachristian.edu/wp-content/uploads/2020/08/AWVI-2020-Release-08-
Perceptions-of-Sin-and-Salvation.pdf

If you step back and look at the big picture painted by all of the outcomes in this research project it seems to suggest that people are in an "anything goes" mindset when it comes to faith, morals, values, and lifestyle. Americans appear to be creating unique, highly customized worldviews based on feelings, experiences and opportunities rather than working within the boundaries of a comprehensive, time-tested, consistent worldview. . . . . If you look at some of the dominant elements in the American mind and heart today, as illuminated by the *Inventory*, we find that most people say that the objective of life is feeling good about yourself; that all faiths are of equal value; that entry into God's eternal presence is determined by one's personal means of choice; and that there are no absolutes to guide or grow us morally. . . . That philosophy of life contradicts a fundamental basis of what may be the two most significant documents to the longevity and success of America—the Bible and the Constitution of the United States. Those documents agree that this nation will only be healthy and fruitful if it is populated by moral people. . . . By abandoning our moral standards and traditions, and replacing them with inclusive and conditional preferences, we are losing the foundations that have enabled the "American experiment" to succeed for more than two centuries. We can only hope that our critical moral institutions—particularly the family and churches—will wake up and help the nation to get back on track.[57]

The Invincibility of the Church

In view of all this, it would seem the church is doomed. But nothing could be further from the truth. God is purging, purifying, and growing His church in precisely the manner He has ordained, and nothing can avert His plan or alter His purposes. In light of Peter's divinely inspired confession (as a representative of the Twelve) that Jesus is "The Christ, the Son of the living God" (Matt. 16:16), Jesus established the foundation of the

---

57   Ibid.

Church saying, "Upon this rock I will build My church; and the gates of Hades will not overpower it" (Matt. 16:18). What great comfort we have in this promise! While the people of the world do not know who Jesus is and do not care, God in His great mercy has revealed this to us. For this reason Jesus said to Peter, "Blessed are you, Simon Barjona, because flesh and blood did not reveal this to you, but My Father who is in heaven" (Matt. 16:17)—a revelation to God's elect that will continue without interruption. Therefore, no matter how bleak the circumstances, how oppressive the enemy, how hopeless the predicament from a human perspective, the Son of God, the Head of the church who cannot lie, will prevail.

We must never lose sight of the fact that it is not *man*, but *Christ* who builds His church (Greek, *ekklēsia*: "the called-out ones"). And He does so through the faithful witness and service of all the Father has given Him (John 6:37)—"as many as the Lord our God shall call to Himself" (Acts 2:39); "as many as [have] been appointed to eternal life [will] [believe]" (Acts 13:48). Every twice-born saint should bow in humble adoration knowing he or she is among the redeemed that God set His unfailing love upon in eternity past! As John MacArthur points out,

> Jesus alluded to the intimacy of the fellowship of believers. "It is My church," He said. As Architect, Builder, Owner, and Lord of His church, Jesus Christ assures His followers that they are His personal possession and eternally have His divine love and care. They are His Body, "purchased with His own blood" (Acts 20:28), and are one with Him in a marvelous, holy intimacy. "The one who joins himself to the Lord is one spirit with Him" (1 Cor. 6:17). Christ is not ashamed to call them "brethren" (Heb. 2:11) and "God is not ashamed to be called their God" (Heb. 11:6). That is why when men attack God's people they attack God Himself. When Jesus confronted Paul (then known as Saul) on the Damascus road, He asked, "Saul, Saul, why are you persecuting Me?" (Acts 9:4). By persecuting Christians (see Acts 8:3; 9:1–2) Saul had been persecuting Christ.

God has always identified Himself with His people and jealously guarded them as His own. He several times referred to His chosen people Israel as the apple, or pupil, of His eye. Through the prophet Zechariah He declared to them, "He who touches you, touches the apple of His eye" (Zech. 2:8; cf. Deut. 32:10; Ps. 17:8; Prov. 7:2). The front part of the eye, the cornea, is the most sensitive exposed part of the human body. God was therefore saying that to harm Israel was to poke a finger in His own eye. To harm God's people is to harm God Himself, and to cause them pain is to cause Him pain.[58]

While Satan's attacks on the church will continue until the Lord returns in judgment, Christ will continue to build it, come what may. Jesus declares the invincibility of His church when He says, "the gates of Hades will not overpower it" (Matt. 16:18)—an idiomatic expression the Jews used frequently for "the powers of death" (based on Isa. 38:10).[59] "Hades" (Hebrew: *sheol*) refers to the place of the departed dead (not hell). It is as if Jesus is saying, "Nothing is strong enough to prevail against My church, not even the power of death that holds My people captive by its gates."

Presently Satan has the power of death, but Christ has rendered him powerless for believers in Christ (Heb. 2:14). Every believer can be certain of Christ's ultimate victory over Satan's power of death because of what He accomplished on the cross: "Since then the children share in flesh and blood, He Himself likewise also partook of the same, that through death He might render powerless him who had the power of death, that is, the devil" (Heb. 2:14). For this reason He comforted the apostle John, and by extension all believers, when He said, "Do not be afraid; I am the first and the last, and the living One; and I was dead, and behold, I am alive forevermore, and I have the keys of death and of Hades" (Rev. 1:18).

---

58   John MacArthur, *The MacArthur New Testament Commentary: Matthew 16–23* (Chicago, Illinois: The Moody Bible Institute of Chicago, 1988), 31–32.

59   C. Blomberg, *Matthew: Vol. 22* (Nashville, Tennessee: Broadman & Holman Publishers, 1992), 253.

"The Blood of the Martyrs is the Seed of the Church"

Though the storm clouds of adversity grow darker, we can find comfort in knowing all things are going according to plan. As I told the discouraged pastor and encouraged him to tell his congregation, these evil days are a wonderful opportunity to trust in God's sovereign rule and purposes to ultimately bring glory to Himself, as He always has and always will. And in these dangerous and uncertain times, God has given us a great opportunity to relax in the agencies of His providence and watch Him orchestrate all the circumstances in our life and country to prove Himself powerful on our behalf. How exciting! And we must never forget that, even in these evil days, Christ is building His church as promised. In fact, persecution is one of His greatest tools.

In autumn of AD 197, Tertullian, one of the Early Church Fathers of the second century, addressed the provincial governors of the Roman Empire in defense of Christianity that was being so unreasonably criticized. There in his work entitled, *Apologeticus*, he coined the phrase, "The blood of martyrs is the seed of the Church." Directly addressing the Roman Empire he boldly declared,

> *We are not a new philosophy but a divine revelation. That's why you can't just exterminate us; the more you kill the more we are. The blood of the martyrs is the seed of the church. You praise those who endured pain and death—so long as they aren't Christians! Your cruelties merely prove our innocence of the crimes you charge against us.... And you frustrate your purpose. Because those who see us die, wonder why we do, for we die like the men you revere, not like slaves or criminals. And when they find out, they join us.*[60]

While persecution against Christians in America doesn't even come close to what the saints have endured in other times and in other places even today, the fact still remains that Christ will build his church and "the gates of Hades will not overpower it" (Matt. 16:16). A great illustration is the growth of the

---

60   http://www.tertullian.org/works/apologeticum.htm

underground church in North Korea, considered by *Open Doors,* an organization serving persecuted Christians in more than sixty countries, "as the most dangerous place in the world to follow Jesus."[61] Kim Chung-seong, a North Korean defector now working as a Christian missionary, says despite the persecution faced by Christians in the world's most difficult place for Christians, the church continues to grow there. He says,

> The one thing that the North Korean regime fears the most, and is afraid of, is the spreading of the Gospel . . . Because the Bible and the Gospel speaks the truth. Once the light shines in the dark room, there is light in the room. . . . They (the government) will do anything to prevent the spread of the Gospel in North Korea. [But] as you can see, we cannot block the sunlight with our hand. . . . Christians are forced to hide their faith completely from government authorities, neighbors and often, even their own spouses and children. Due to ever-present surveillance, many pray with eyes open, and gathering for praise or fellowship is practically impossible . . . . Worship of the ruling Kim family is mandated for all citizens, and those who don't comply (including Christians) are arrested, imprisoned, tortured or killed. Entire Christian families are imprisoned in hard labor camps, where unknown numbers die each year from torture, beatings, overexertion and starvation. Those who attempt to flee to South Korea through China risk execution or life imprisonment, and those who stay behind often fare no better.[62]

Longing for Glory

Though "the sufferings of Christ are ours in abundance" (2 Cor. 1:5), we can find relief knowing that Satan's rule is only temporary and our glorious King will one day return in power and great glory to put at an end once and for all to evil and suffering. The tragedies

---

61   https://www.opendoorsuk.org/persecution/world-watch-list/north-korea/#:~:text=Open%20Doors%20estimates%20that%20there%20are%20approximately%20300%2C000,imprisoned%20in%20terrible%20labour%20camps%20for%20their%20faith.

62   https://www.christianpost.com/news/christianity-growing-in-north-korea-despite-persecution-defector-says.html

and atrocities of life should animate our hatred of Satan and sin, and never incite our anger toward God. The inevitable sorrows of life in this sin-cursed world are opportunities for us to long all the more for glory when "He will wipe away every tear from [our] eyes; and there will no longer be any death; there will no longer be any mourning, or crying, or pain; the first things have passed away" (Rev. 21:4). But until that glorious day, we can find comfort knowing that God has not abandoned us in our sufferings. For indeed, in His permissive providence He has ordained to allow them to accomplish His eternal purpose to bring glory to Himself and eternal life to those He has saved by His grace.

Through life's storms we must trust our glorious God for who He is, for His goodness and justice remain untarnished in all that He does. Moses said, "The Rock! His work is perfect, for all His ways are just; a God of faithfulness and without injustice, righteous and upright is He" (Deut. 32:4). He is the thrice-holy God praised by the seraphim (Isa. 6:3)—holiness being the all-encompassing attribute of God that portrays His hidden glory, His infinite otherness, His incomprehensible transcendence, His consummate perfection, and His moral purity. For this reason, the apostle John says, "God is Light, and in Him there is no darkness at all" (1 John 1:5). And it is only in Him that we can find light in the darkness of evil.

For this reason, Peter comforted the persecuted saints when he said, "Humble yourselves under the mighty hand of God, that He may exalt you at the proper time, casting all your anxiety on Him, because He cares for you" (1 Peter 5:7–6). Even in the hopelessness and helplessness of excruciating sorrow and gratuitous evil, we can rest assured in God's promise that He will never leave us nor forsake us (Heb. 13:5). Moreover, when we look closely, in every trial we can see His tender mercies and goodness put on display, often in ways that are unexpected—a glimpse of the glory to come. And then, in the midst of the pain, we will find comfort and experience the soul-satisfying joy of His presence, consistent with His promise that He will never give us more than we can bear (1 Cor. 10:13), His grace will always be sufficient (2 Cor. 12:9), and His throne is always accessible. "Therefore let us draw near with confidence to the throne of grace, so that we may receive mercy and find grace to help in time of need" (Heb. 4:16).

Truly, "the Lord's lovingkindnesses indeed never cease, for His compassions never fail. They are new every morning; Great is Your faithfulness" (Lam. 3:22–23). In light of these great truths, we can affirm the inspired words of James when he says: "Consider it all joy, my brethren, when you encounter various trials, knowing that the testing of your faith produces endurance. And let endurance have its perfect result, so that you may be perfect and complete, lacking in nothing" (James 1:2–4).

Armed with these great truths, and comforted by them, our heart can echo the apostle's great doxology of faith and say:

> Oh, the depth of the riches both of the wisdom and knowledge of God! How unsearchable are His judgments and unfathomable His ways!
> For who has known the mind of the Lord, or who became His counselor?
> Or who has first given to Him that it might be paid back to him again?
> For from Him and through Him and to Him are all things.
> To Him be the glory forever. Amen.
> (Rom. 11:33)

Final Words of Encouragement

Without a doubt, America's growing disdain for biblical Christianity is troubling, and the satanically inspired policies of Democratic Socialists target all that we hold dear for the glory of Christ. But our great assurance is that our God reigns in absolute sovereignty over His creation and His purposes cannot be frustrated— although they will include difficulties even for those He loves. For He has declared, "I am the LORD, there is no other. Besides Me there is no God . . . The One forming light and creating darkness, causing well-being and creating calamity; I am the LORD who does all these" (Isa. 45:5, 7).

But because of Christ's sacrificial death on our behalf, "God highly exalted Him, and bestowed on Him the name which is above every name, so that at the name of Jesus every knee will bow, of those who are in heaven and on earth and under the earth, and that every tongue will confess that Jesus Christ is Lord, to the glory of God the Father" (Phil. 2:9–11). And with utmost confidence we will one day be among the great gathering of the redeemed described in Revelation 7:9–12:

> I looked, and behold, a great multitude which no one could count, from every nation and all tribes and peoples and tongues, standing before the throne and before the Lamb, clothed in white robes, and palm branches were in their hands; and they cry out with a loud voice, saying, "Salvation to our God who sits on the throne, and to the Lamb." And all the angels were standing around the throne and around the elders and the four living creatures; and they fell on their faces before the throne and worshiped God, saying, "Amen, blessing and glory and wisdom and thanksgiving and honor and power and might, be to our God forever and ever. Amen."

May we all be deeply encouraged by these inspired and exhilarating truths.

7

. . . .

The Christian's Ambition

Pursuing the Prize of Christlikeness

*I press on so that I may lay hold of that for which also I was
laid hold of by Christ Jesus.*

Philippians 3:12

Any honest observer must admit that a strange mixture of nihilism and dogmatism dominates our postmodern, post-Christian American culture. *Nihilism* denies the existence of moral truth and considers our very existence to be senseless and useless, while *dogmatism* is characterized by an inflexible opinion of a particular belief or set of beliefs considered to be true beyond question.

Although the cultural elites are absolutely certain that absolute certainty does not exist in the realm of morality or religion, they have, nevertheless, proudly created their own societal orthodoxies and hold to them with fierce intransigence. For example, neo-Marxist political ideologies, Critical Race Theory, and LGBTQ morality are sacrosanct; they are absolute truths! In the minds of those who hold them, any challenge must therefore be met with fierce opposition, and any competing points of view must never be allowed an audience. This is why America's Constitutional freedoms of speech and religion are constantly being undermined. Yet these same people will categorically dismiss Christian doctrine because they insist absolute truth is unknowable, unless, of course, it is their truth.

Suppressing the Truth in Unrighteousness

From a Christian perspective, the problem with this kind of group-think schizophrenia is that it not only enslaves people to Satan's kingdom of darkness, but it also violates their consciences, producing within them a gnawing sense of doubt and guilt. "For the wrath of God is revealed from heaven against all ungodliness and unrighteousness of men who suppress the truth in unrighteousness, because that which is known about God is evident within them; for God made it evident to them" (Rom. 1:18–19). This is why non-Christians are so defensive about their "truth" and so hostile to the gospel. Truth has a way of prying the lid off the crate of lies they so desperately try to conceal. As Lenski puts it,

> To suppress, [is] to prevent the truth from exerting its power in the heart and the life. The truth is not merely quietly held while men go on in immorality, for it is the nature of truth to

exert itself, make its power felt; it is held down so that it shall not exert itself. . . . despite the constant revelation of God's wrath, men go on in their wickedness: whenever the truth starts to exert itself and makes them feel uneasy in their moral nature, they hold it down, suppress it. . . . *Aléthia* is "truth" in the sense of "reality," that which is actually so. The context points especially to God and to his wrath against all ungodliness and unrighteousness. Instead of allowing this truth its proper control in their hearts men hold it down. That, of course, is all they are able to do. They are not able to destroy this or any other reality. Truth quietly remains what it is amid all the clamor and the shouting against it and in the end judges every man. Woe to him who has refused to yield to it his heart and his life![63]

This is the sad plight of the unregenerate who reject the light of the gospel of Christ in order to pursue their lusts (John 3:19). The result is self-imposed spiritual darkness, especially as it relates to the wrath of God that awaits them. They "walk in the futility of their mind, being darkened in their understanding, excluded from the life of God because of the ignorance that is in them, because of the hardness of their heart; and they, having become callous, have given themselves over to sensuality for the practice of every kind of impurity with greediness" (Eph. 4:17–19). They are "strangers to the covenants of promise, having no hope and without God in the world" (Eph. 2:12).

And when these people are placed in authority over a nation, the results are catastrophic. Just look at what has happened in cities controlled by Democrats. No wonder so many people are leaving them in droves. Yet millions of others see no problem. It's as if they live in a parallel universe. They actually vote their own destruction—evidence of self-imposed moral and spiritual blindness. And this is what Christian people are sensing like never before in our lifetime. This is verification of the Satanic "fortresses . . . speculations and every lofty thing raised up against the knowledge of God" (2 Cor. 10:4–5); a reference to the satanic assaults on the gospel—the message of divine mercy and grace that America hates.

---

63 R. C. H. Lenski, *The Interpretation of St. Paul's Epistle to the Romans* (Columbus, Ohio: Lutheran Book Concern, 1936), 92–93.

A Life without Meaning and Purpose

It's tragic to watch this play out, especially in the lives of young people who increasingly admit to a lack of meaning and purpose in life. Yet they desperately try to find them in a Satanically controlled world that seeks their eternal destruction and will one day pass away in the fiery wrath of divine judgment. Many complain of having feelings of emptiness, loneliness, hopelessness, guilt, fear, and depression. This is part of the reason illicit drug use is so rampant. The COVID pandemic has exacerbated the situation, according to a CDC report, causing an increasing number of Generation Zers and millennials to resort to substance abuse to cope with stress and anxiety.[64]

> Forty percent of American adults are struggling with mental health issues or substance abuse, according to the U.S. Center for Disease Control and Prevention's most recent *Morbidity and Mortality Weekly Report*. Of particular concern is the percentage of young adults having suicidal thoughts. One in four Americans ages 18–24 considered suicide within the past month, according to a survey completed by 5,412 adults between June 24 and June 30. So did 16% of respondents ages 25–44. Nearly 25% of adults ages 18–24 said they have started or increased substance abuse to cope with pandemic-related stress or emotions. About 63% reported having an anxiety or depressive disorder. The situation was only marginally better among the next age group. About 40% of adults ages 25–44 had an anxiety or depressive disorder. About 20% had started or increased substance abuse.[65]

Notwithstanding the effects of the pandemic lockdown, many unsaved young adults I have talked with are quite nervous about their future and in varying ways express how they really don't have much to live for—the nihilism described earlier. Their identity as a man or woman has nothing to do with the *imago Dei* (Latin: "image of God"). They give no consideration

---

64   https://www.phillyvoice.com/mental-health-statistics-covid-19-generation-z-millennials-suicide-substance-abuse/

65   Ibid.

to the fact that they were made in the image of God (Gen. 1:26–28), or in what specifically does that image actually consist. Nor do they consider how sin and the fall of man have marred that image and how the benefits of the redemptive work of Christ accrues to the image of sinful men and women who put their trust in Him.

For the unregenerate, personal identity is self-perceived. It is solely dependent on *who* or *what* they want to be, how they see themselves, and how they want others to see them. This is how they find meaning and self-fulfillment in life—or so they think. Some seek a sense of personal satisfaction in their career, or becoming a social justice warrior or a global warming activist or neo-Marxist revolutionary, or some other grandiose world-saving quest. But in the end—and often long before—they realize nothing ever satisfied the longings of their soul.

A Crisis in Identity

This is because no one can escape reality. No one can hide from God. No one can successfully deny or eradicate the *imago Dei*. No one can squelch the fear of impending judgment. All they can do is try (in vain) to "suppress the truth in unrighteousness" (Rom. 1:18). But try as they may, in the middle of the night, when all is quiet and they're all alone, those feelings of emptiness, loneliness, hopelessness, guilt, fear, and depression haunt them like a ghost in the darkness. The irresistible force of truth that there is a God who created them, and He will one day judge them exerts itself upon their conscience once again. But rather than pleading for the undeserved mercy and grace so readily available to all who repent, they try to find some way to silence their accusing conscience. And the world offers many ways to make it all go away, at least temporarily.

Why do you think our culture has fought so hard to legalize marijuana despite the devastating effects it's having on people's minds, bodies, and society in general? Why do you think illicit drug abuse and alcohol addiction is so widespread in our society? Here's a sample of some of the prevailing "conscience silencing" remedies the culture recommends this:

When your conscience suddenly hits you with those phony feelings of guilt and fear, you know, that superstitious stuff about being alienated from the life of God and knowing in your heart of hearts that judgment awaits you when you die, the best thing to do is smoke another joint. Or if that doesn't work, pour another drink, or watch another movie, or turn up the volume on your favorite music, or search the internet for some porn, or escape into cyber-world where no one really knows you. Oh, and while you're there, update your profile picture (again) with one of your latest "selfies." Also, post some of your profound wisdom on social media to advance whatever cause you're into.

Impress people with how smart you are. Do something to draw attention to yourself and garner some more "likes." Oh, and by the way, make sure you bash those idiotic Christian bigots and homophobes; we've get to keep them in their place, you know. They're part of the reason you're feeling so out of sorts. Then take a pill to help you get back to sleep so you can make it to work. After all, you've got to make enough money to retire on and enjoy life, because remember, life is short, make the most of it. Live for yourself. After all, your happiness is all that really matters in life. Like they say, "Eat, drink, and be merry, for tomorrow we die."

That's the *American Dream* for those without Christ. They live for themselves in self-imposed moral and spiritual darkness, and then they die, all the while doing whatever it takes to keep "[suppressing] the truth in unrighteousness" (Rom. 1:18). This illustrates Solomon's ancient analysis of people's depraved condition when he declared, "The hearts of the sons of men are full of evil, and insanity is in their hearts throughout their lives" (Eccl. 9:3). How radically different all this is from the life of those who are united to Christ in saving faith. Yet we're hated because of it.

Man is selfish and self-willed by nature. He has an identity crisis. He not only demands to be noticed, but also to be worshipped. Facebook capitalizes on this reality. Most users are desperate for affirmation and assume everyone wants to know the intimate details of their life, the wisdom of their intellects, and the beauty of their body. Facebook would fold up within twenty-four hours if it removed the "likes" option.

This is also one of the driving forces in the social justice movement that so many in the evangelical church fail to understand. Darrell B. Harrison makes this observation:

> Unlike previous embracements of this ideology by the church—because there is truly nothing new under the sun (Eccl. 1:9)—this current adoration of the social gospel seems especially occupied and absorbed with the idea of personal identity. That is, a self-focused desire to be acknowledged and, perhaps even admired, not for who we are in Christ (Col. 3:1–3) but for who we are in ourselves and in what makes us unique apart from Him.[66]

This is why the social activism and the social justice gospel are so impotent. Neither is capable of changing a person's heart. Moreover, what a hollow victory to gain affirmation by force; worse yet, what a meaningless existence to be praised by people for a few short years on earth yet be separated from God for eternity. "For what does it profit a man to gain the whole world, and forfeit his soul?" (Mark 8:36).

The Christian's Identity

The most basic aspect of salvation is the Christian's *union with Christ*—"that there is . . . no condemnation for those who are in Christ Jesus" (Rom. 8:1); that "if any man is in Christ, he is a new creature" (2 Cor. 5:17). *His life alone* satisfied the righteous demands of the Law, *not His plus mine*—consistent with Paul's desire to "be found in Him, not having a righteousness of my own derived from the Law, but that which is through faith in Christ, the righteousness which comes from God on the basis of faith" (Phil. 3:9). Therefore, God no longer sees our sin; instead, He sees the righteousness of His beloved Son, "for [I] have died and [my] life

---

66 https://www.christianpost.com/voices/the-fault-in-their-social-gospel.html

is hidden with Christ in God" (Col. 3:3); "For He has clothed me with garments of salvation, He has wrapped me with a robe of righteousness" (Isa. 61:10). Therefore, *we are in permanent possession of all that is His.*

The Christian finds his or her identity in Christ alone. He is our life, our joy, our hope, and our power. Because the "Father of our Lord Jesus Christ . . . has blessed us with every spiritual blessing in the heavenly places in Christ" (Eph. 1:3). We are "a temple of the living God" (2 Cor. 6:16), and "His divine power has granted to us everything pertaining to life and godliness" (2 Peter 1:3). Because we are united to Christ, we are able to "[strive] according to His power, which mightily works within [us]" (Col. 1:29) because He alone "is able to do exceeding abundantly beyond all that we ask or think, according to the power that works within us"(Eph. 3:20).

Christ Our All-Glorious End

Many professing Christians in America see belief in Jesus Christ as a way of getting their ticket punched for heaven, when, in reality, *Christ is not a means to an end, but He is the all-sufficient and all-glorious end Himself.* Christ esteemed this profound reality so highly that it was the primary emphasis in His High Priestly prayer to His Father as He prepared to endure the agonies of the cross on our behalf. He prayed

> that they may all be one; even as You, Father, are in Me and I in You, that they also may be in Us, so that the world may believe that You sent Me. The glory which You have given Me I have given to them, that they may be one, just as We are one; I in them and You in Me, that they may be perfected in unity, so that the world may know that You sent Me, and loved them, even as You have loved Me.
> (John 17:21–23)

It is impossible to fathom the gulf that exists between our holy Creator and His sinful creatures. For the Son of God to purchase our redemption and be married to such a wretched bride is equally unfathomable. Nevertheless, such was the intended unity decreed before the foundation of the world; and it was this very union between Christ and all whom the Father had given Him that occupied the heart of our Lord on the eve of His crucifixion. That this is recorded in Scripture is certain proof that He wants all who belong to Him to accurately apprehend the nature of this mystical union so that we might esteem it as He did. It was His desire for His bridal church to relish the profound implications of this everlasting marriage, so that she might enjoy the staggering benefits of what it means to be "in Christ"—theology that is virtually unheard of in America today.

This is also at the heart of Paul's doxology recorded in Ephesians 1:3: "Blessed be the God and Father of our Lord Jesus Christ, who has blessed us with every spiritual blessing in the heavenly places in Christ." That little preposition "in" ("in Christ") signifies the deep wonder of Christ being more than *with* us, more than existing *outside* us, but One who is *in* us, and we are *in* Him. He is One who is *more* than our sovereign King, our risen Savior, our Lord and Master, teacher or friend, although He is all this and more!

To be "in Christ" is not some mystical form of *pantheism* where Christ is absorbed into the "wholeness" which is God; nor is it a *physical* union (as taught by Sacramentarians) where Christ enters men physically by participating in some rite or ceremony; nor is it a union of *essence* where we lose our human identity and become one with God or absorbed into Christ. Rather, it is an expression of interconnectedness whereby we share a common spiritual life with Him, for "[we] have died and [our] life is hidden with Christ in God" (Col. 3:3). He is "our life" (Col. 3:4), and He lives in us (Gal. 2:20).

Scripture reveals some amazing truths about the nature of this union.

- It is a *supernatural union* authored by God: "If anyone loves Me, he will keep My word; and My Father will love him, and We will come to him and make Our abode with him" (John 14:23).
- It is a *vital union* by which Christ becomes our very life: "I have been crucified with Christ; and it is no longer I who

live, but Christ lives in me; and the life which I now live in the flesh I live by faith in the Son of God, who loved me and gave Himself up for me" (Gal. 2:20; *cf.* Col. 3:3–4).

- It is an *organic union* in that with Christ believers form one body (the church) and respond to Christ as the head: "He is . . . the head of the body, the church" (Col. 1:18; *cf.* 1 Cor. 12:4–27; Eph. 4:15; 5:23).
- It is a *spiritual union* in that Christ dwells within us by the Spirit who is the Spirit of Christ (1 Peter 1:11; *cf.* Rom. 8:9; 2 Cor. 3:18); "for by one Spirit we were all baptized into one body . . . and we were all made to drink of one Spirit" (1 Cor. 12:13).
- It is a *legal union* in that Christ is our representative head who has made us the beneficiary of his substitutionary work of salvation: "So then as through one transgression there resulted condemnation to all men, even so through one act of righteousness there resulted justification of life to all men. For as through the one man's disobedience the many were made sinners, even so through the obedience of the One the many will be made righteous" (Rom. 5:18–19).
- It is a *mysterious union* in that it has no analogy in human experience: "God willed to make known what is the riches of the glory of this mystery among the Gentiles, which is Christ in you, the hope of glory" (Col. 1:27).
- It is an *everlasting union* that can never be severed: "For I am convinced that neither death, nor life, nor angels, nor principalities, nor things present, nor things to come, nor powers, nor height, nor depth, nor any other created thing, will be able to separate us from the love of God, which is in Christ Jesus our Lord" (Rom. 8:38–39).

The Holy Spirit helps us grasp this unfathomable mystery by describing it through various figures.

- We are "married" to Christ (Rom. 7:4).
- We are to Christ as a bride is to a bridegroom (Eph. 5:22–23).
- We are branches on the true vine (John 15:1–11).
- We partake of Jesus, the true bread from heaven (John 6:51).

- We are the body and Jesus is the head (Eph. 1:22–23).
- We are a spiritual building "joined together, and [growing] into a holy temple in the Lord" (Eph. 2:21).

The implications of these descriptions are staggering, not only as they relate to the doctrine of salvation, but also how we as believers actually live out this union in our gospel proclamation, worship, service, and relationships with other believers. I stand in awe when I reflect upon the glorious reality that Jesus Christ came to this earth not only to pay the penalty for my sin, but also to establish an intimate, living, eternal union with me whereby I become one with Him. I trust you share my amazement, and my eternal gratitude and joy!

The Need for Union with Christ

Unlike the doctrinally weak and politically correct sermon-ettes that are heard in most churches these days, what must be preached is *a sober recognition of the terrifying separation that exists between our Holy God and fallen man that makes union with Christ an indispensable necessity for salvation.* How many professing Christians really understand this? This is especially so of those in seek-er-sensitive churches where the sermons are as shallow as water on a plate. It has been my observation based upon conversations with hundreds of believers over the years that very few comprehend the chasm that has been bridged through their union with Christ. Like the average American, most don't see themselves as all that sinful—nor do they see God as all that holy; and most don't really understand how Christ fits into the picture, especially as it relates to their union with Him.

Yet we see this explained repeatedly in the New Testament. For example, the apostle Paul reminded the saints in Colossae that before they were saved, they were "alienated and hostile in mind, engaged in evil deeds, yet He has now reconciled you in His fleshly body through death, in order to present you before Him holy and blameless and beyond reproach" (Col. 1:21–22). Likewise, Paul reminded the Gentile saints at Ephesus that before their salvation, they were once alienated, "separate from Christ, excluded from the commonwealth of Israel, and strangers to the covenants of promise, having no hope and without God in the world" (Eph. 2:12). But then, in contrast to this great horror, Paul states the remedy for our estrangement is based upon our union with Christ, saying, "But now *in Christ Jesus* you who formerly were far off have been brought near by the blood of Christ" (Eph. 2:13; emphasis mine).

Because we are united to Christ, we are no longer controlled by our fallen flesh, though sometimes we sinfully succumb to it: "For those who are according to the flesh set their minds on the things of the flesh, but those who are according to the Spirit, the things of the Spirit" (Rom. 8:5). The life of an unbeliever, however, is dominated by the fallen, sinful nature with which he or she was born. Unbelievers live under the authority of their *flesh*—a reference to sinful man's moral inadequacy contained in his unredeemed humanness, his innate inability to conform to the righteous character and desires of God.

What a powerful indictment this is! To "set their minds" upon something is to give continuous and serious consideration to it. It means to ponder, to let one's mind dwell upon, to fix one's attention upon something. It is all they think about. Those who are living according to the flesh are bound in their thoughts to the desires of the flesh such as "immorality, impurity, sensuality, idolatry, sorcery, enmities, strife, jealousy, outbursts of anger, disputes, dissensions, factions, envying, drunkenness, carousing, and the things like these, of which I forewarned you just as I have forewarned you that those who practice such things shall not inherit the kingdom of God" (Gal. 5:19–21). Peter also described the unregenerate person as one who seeks to "indulge the flesh in its corrupt desires" (2 Peter 2:10). To the Philippians, Paul wrote, "[They are those] whose end is destruction, whose god is their appetite, and whose glory is in their shame, who set their minds on earthly things" (Phil. 3:19).

It is important to note what Paul did *not* say in Romans 8:5. He did *not* say, "For the mind that is set on the flesh *leads* to death." He said that it "*is* death." What does he mean? He means an unbeliever is alive physically, but he is *dead spiritually*. He is a spiritual cadaver. The unregenerate man lives in the realm of the damned. The wrath of God abides upon him. Because of the offense of his sin against a holy God, he is doomed to eternal death. And that which is dead cannot respond unless God does something! Unless God Himself initiates the process of a complete redemption, there is none.

Indeed, unless God breathes spiritual life into the sinner, his mind remains set on the flesh. In Romans 8:7 Paul goes on to say, "The mind set on the flesh is hostile toward God; for it does not subject itself to the law of God, for it is not even able to do so." The walking dead love their sin more than they love God. They live for all this world can offer them. They do not subject themselves to the law of God, and they are unable to do so. Apart from the regenerating grace of the Holy Spirit that baptizes them *into* Christ, they will remain forever alienated from God. And only the new birth can initiate this union—"But God, being rich in mercy, because of His great love with which He loved us, even when we were dead in our transgressions, made us alive together with Christ" (Eph. 2:4).

The Gospel Offer of Christ Himself

I often find my heart captivated by the magnitude of God's grace in justification by faith alone, despite my sin. Paul expresses this when he says: "There is now no condemnation for those who are *in* Christ Jesus" (Rom. 8:1; emphasis mine). This is a truly astonishing passage of Scripture, allowing us to behold the grandeur and mystery of the gospel of God. Here again we see that the gospel offer of salvation is not a gift of grace that comes *through* Christ; it *is* Christ. He *is* the gospel. None of the benefits of saving grace exist separately from Him, but only *in* Him. For this reason, we can rejoice with Paul and say, "Blessed be the God and Father of our Lord Jesus Christ, who has blessed us with every spiritual blessing in the heavenly places in Christ" (Eph. 1:3).

While this is the only truth that saves (Rom. 1:16), many professing Christians fail to understand it. According to a Pew Research Center survey, 52 percent of Protestants in the United States say that "both good deeds and faith are needed to get into heaven, a historically Catholic belief." Such lack of clarity on the most basic element of saving grace emphasizes the need for fearless preachers to stand up and "[proclaim] . . . the testimony of God" and, like the apostle Paul, be willing to say to the Corinthians of our day, "I determined to know nothing among you except Jesus Christ, and Him crucified" (1 Cor. 2:1–2).

But this is seldom the case these days. As a result, the glorious gospel offer of *Christ Himself* has been hijacked by clever perversions like the *prosperity gospel* that would have us believe Christ died to make us happy, or the *social justice gospel* that requires the church to advocate for Critical Race Theory and embrace a cultural definition of justice that is always changing and that has nothing to do with the justice of God. Fighting against such distortions (and there are many others), Paul warned, "If anyone preaches to you a gospel contrary to that which we have preached to you, let him be accursed" (Gal. 1:8).

Although many subtle and some not-so-subtle doctrinal aberrations can lead to a false gospel, neglecting the doctrine of a believer's union with Christ must be among the most dangerous. The pervasive ignorance concerning it and the concomitant apathy toward it prove how it has been disregarded. For this reason, it is important to reacquaint the true church with the same truths the apostle Paul reminded the saints at Ephesus—*that were it not for the union of God's elect in Christ, we would perish in our sins.* Indeed, we would still be "dead in our trespasses and sins . . . [walking] according to the course of this world, according to the prince of the power of the air, of the spirit that is now working in the sons of disobedience. . . indulging the desires of the flesh and of the mind, and . . . by nature children of wrath, even as the rest" (Eph. 2:1–3).

This is what makes our union with Christ so glorious. This is what makes the gospel such amazingly good news, because saving grace is more than a gift made available *through* Christ; *it is Christ Himself!* Because we are united to Him, we have "peace with God" (Rom. 5:1) which allows us to pass through the veil of separation and have *access to God.* Through our Lord Jesus Christ, "we have obtained our introduction by faith into this grace in which we stand" (Rom. 5:2).

Pursuing the Prize of Christlikeness

....

These are fundamental truths of the gospel that have been ne-
glected by a cultural Christianity that is more concerned about
being *popular* than being *faithful.* The exclusivity of Christ doesn't
sell well in our culture. But it is the only truth that saves and sanc-
tifies. Much of the chaos in our country can be attributed to the
appalling compromise of evangelical leaders who simply refuse
to preach the Word with unflinching boldness despite the world's
hatred of it (2 Tim. 4:2).

When Paul came to the wicked city of Corinth, his message was
uncompromising and his manner was *unconventional.* His strategies
for church growth made no sense from the world's perspective.
Remember, his message is summarized in one powerful
statement: "For I determined to know nothing among you except
Jesus Christ, and Him crucified" (1 Cor. 2:2). He understood what
many today seem to forget, and that is, the message of the gospel
is the only message God uses to utterly transform sinners into
the likeness of Christ. Though it is a stumbling block to the Jews
and foolishness to the Greeks, "to those who are the called, both
Jews and Greeks," it is "Christ the power of God and the wisdom of
God" (1 Cor. 1:23–24). And because of this, Paul gave the following
testimony that should be echoed by every believer:

> I count all things to be loss in view of the surpassing value of
> knowing Christ Jesus my Lord, for whom I have suffered the
> loss of all things, and count them but rubbish so that I may
> gain Christ, and may be found in Him, not having a righ-
> teousness of my own derived from the Law, but that which is
> through faith in Christ, the righteousness which comes from
> God on the basis of faith, that I may know Him and the pow-
> er of His resurrection and the fellowship of His sufferings,
> being conformed to His death; in order that I may attain to
> the resurrection from the dead. Not that I have already ob-
> tained it or have already become perfect, but I press on so
> that I may lay hold of that for which also I was laid hold of
> by Christ Jesus. Brethren, I do not regard myself as having
> laid hold of it yet; but one thing I do: forgetting what lies

behind and reaching forward to what lies ahead, I press on toward the goal for the prize of the upward call of God in Christ Jesus.
(Phil. 3:8–14)

Because we are united to Christ, we are in permanent possession of all that is His. For this reason, all that we *have* and *are* on earth is nothing in comparison. Despite his Jewish pedigree and impeccable credentials as a Pharisee, Paul "[counted] all things to be loss in view of the surpassing value of knowing Christ Jesus [his] Lord" (v. 8). Every believer understands this. The exhilarating presence of Christ within us produces a soul-satisfying joy that exceeds all others in this life, a little taste of heaven. For indeed, *Christ is not a means to an end; He is the all-sufficient and all-glorious end Himself.* As a result, those who truly love Him and know Him experientially enjoy the unrestricted rule of the Spirit of God in their heart. They enjoy a transcendent, personal, experiential communion with Him as expressed by Paul's use of *gnōsis* (translated "knowing" [v. 8] and "to know" [v. 10]).

Paul's greatest ambition was to exert all his energy to know more of Christ, to experience more of His resurrection power, to enjoy Him more fully, and become more like Him no matter the cost. For this reason he says, "I press on toward the goal for the prize of the upward call of God in Christ Jesus" (v. 14). And what was that prize that motivated him to win (1 Cor. 9:24)? What was his life's ambition? *Christlikeness!* This was a prize he would not ultimately attain fully until "the upward call of God in Christ Jesus" (v. 14) when he would see his Savior and Lord face-to-face in the splendor of heaven. And it is the pursuit of Christlikeness that should motivate every believer.

This was Christ's goal in saving us in the first place, as Paul reveals in Romans 8:29: "For those whom He foreknew, He also predestined to become conformed to the image of His Son, so that He would be the firstborn among many brethren." Therefore it should also be our goal in Christians living: "It was for this He called you through our gospel, that you may gain the glory of our Lord Jesus Christ" (2 Thess. 2:14).

A Time for Full Exertion and Authoritative Exhortation

For many years life in America has been good. We've enjoyed unprecedented freedom and prosperity. But when times are easy, Christians grow complacent. Like the rest of our culture, as long as we have good health and healthcare, a decent job, money in the bank, high-speed Internet, cable TV, and our favorite sports team is winning, we're happy. But we're also growing weaker in our faith, becoming insensitive to our sin, and our love for Christ begins to wane. Our hearts are drawn to other lovers—materialism, entertainment, hobbies, and a host of other objects that garner our affection. We stop exerting ourselves to go hard after Christ. We stop "[pressing] on so that [we] may lay hold of that for which also [we] were laid hold of by Christ Jesus" (Phil. 3:12). We stop "striving according to His power" (Col. 1:29) and the fruit of the Spirit grows sickly on the vine of our life (Gal. 5:22–23). We no longer "Fight the good fight of faith; take hold of the eternal life to which [we] were called" (1 Tim. 6:12).

And when our loving heavenly Father sees this, He often brings trouble in our life. And like never before in my lifetime, that trouble is here in our country! This is a time for full exertion. This is a time to pursue the prize of Christlikeness like never before. This is time to know Him and the power of His resurrection in ways that we have never even imagined. It's time to be bold in our gospel preaching and godly in our gospel living.

To these ends I wish to encourage every Christian reader with some further truths relating to our union with Christ that are essential for us to understand and apply if indeed we are going to pursue the prize of Christlikeness amidst the moral free fall in our country. I must also add that I'm burdened to share these things because of the unprecedented spiritual hunger I am currently observing in the sphere of my ministry as a pastor. People are starving for biblical truth. They're craving the glory and greatness of God revealed in His Word, making it all the more incumbent upon all ministers of the gospel to "speak the things which are fitting for sound doctrine" (Titus 2:1). "Speak and exhort and reprove with all authority. Let no one disregard you" (Titus 2:15).

A Temple of the Living God

First, we must remember: *the fruit of authentic regeneration and union with Christ is a life of joyful and habitual obedience motivated by a sincere love for Christ.* For the most part, this is seldom seen in modern evangelicalism. It is this visible proof that constitutes an *objective* assurance of our salvation while at the same time confirming the *subjective*, internal witness of the Holy Spirit (1 John 5:10; Rom. 8:14–16; 2 Cor. 1:12). Furthermore—and this is incomprehensible—because of our union with Christ we are also united to the Father and the Holy Spirit as He is (John 10:30). Indeed, "we are a temple of the living God" (2 Cor. 6:16), "[we] are built together into a dwelling of God in the Spirit" (Eph. 2:22), our "life is hidden with Christ in God" (Col. 3:3). And because of this Jesus says, "If anyone loves Me, he will keep My word; and My Father will love him, and We will come to him and make Our abode with him" (John 14:23).

The implications of this ineffable union as they relate to life and godliness cannot be overemphasized. That the Triune Godhead dwells within His redeemed people explains the God-exalting disposition and supernatural resources they possess to cause them to bear the fruit of righteousness for the glory of God. This, of course, is in contrast to the apostate Christian who is only superficially attached to the vine—Christ—and is therefore a non-fruit-bearing branch that must be removed and burned, a subject we will now consider.

In John 15:4–5 Jesus made this amazing statement:

> Abide in Me, and I in you. As the branch cannot bear fruit of itself unless it abides in the vine, so neither can you unless you abide in Me. I am the vine, you are the branches; he who abides in Me and I in him, he bears much fruit, for apart from Me you can do nothing.

In light of Jesus' statement and a believer's union with Christ, we can define a Christian as *one in whom the Triune Godhead dwells eternally, empowering that individual to manifest the fruit of His righteousness for His glory.* Notice closely what Jesus says.

He begins by saying, "I am the true vine" (John 15:1). This is the last of the "I am" (Greek: *ego eimi*) declarations where Jesus asserts His deity and His saving relationship toward the world. The title, "I am" bears the Old Testament divine name of LORD[67] Yahweh, the same title of deity disclosed to Moses at the burning bush in Exodus 3:14. Previously in John 8, Jesus infuriated the Pharisees by declaring Himself to be the LORD, the same LORD of the Old Testament, when He said to them, "Truly, truly, I say to you, before Abraham was born, I am" (v. 58). This was also the infinitely powerful declaration of Himself that caused the soldiers, officers, and Judas himself to fall helplessly to the ground when they came to arrest Him (John 18:6).

Abiding in Jesus—the True Vine

That Jesus claimed to be the LORD, "the true vine," was of utmost importance, because in the Old Testament the vine symbolized Israel, the covenant people of God (Ps. 80:9–16; Isa. 5:1–7; 37:2ff; Jer. 2:21; 12:10ff; Ezek. 15:1–8; 17:1–21; 19:10–14; Hos. 10:1–2). But as these references indicate, the vine's failure to produce good fruit was a harbinger of divine judgment upon the nation. It also pointed to the need of a "true vine" that would bring forth good fruit, namely Jesus their Messiah. Throughout Jesus' ministry, He confronted the misplaced trust the Jewish people had in their heritage to save them. They mistakenly believed that simply because they were born of the seed of Abraham and were therefore people of the covenant, they were automatically united to God and the only deserving recipients of His blessing. But in reality, apart from faith in Jesus their Messiah, "the true vine" (John 15:1) and source of all spiritual blessings and godliness (John 1:5), they remained alienated from God and unable to produce the fruit of righteousness that can only flow through Him.

Jesus also wanted His disciples to understand that only those connected to the "true vine" by genuine saving faith (unlike many in Israel, and unlike Judas) were the recipients of divine blessing, validated by their fruit of righteousness (John 15:4). He made the

---

67 The Name of God rendered in small capitals, LORD, is explained in the incident of Moses encountering God at the burning bush in Exodus 3.1–15. Most Bible versions simply render it typographically as LORD; a few render it as Jehovah or as Yahweh.

same assertion earlier in John 14:6 when He said, "I am the way, and the truth, and the life; no one comes to the Father but through Me." So when Jesus said, "I am the true vine" (v. 1), He was not only asserting His deity ("I am") but also, because He is the "true vine," He was the perfect, genuine, complete, and essential vine, in contradistinction to the vine of Israel that "He expected . . . to produce good grapes, but it produced only worthless ones" (Isa. 5:2). Judas was a living illustration of just that.

Like so many over the course of redemptive history, including our modern era, many people have a superficial attachment to Jesus due to a meaningless, insincere profession of faith or a mere church affiliation. "Nevertheless," as Carson aptly states, "by failing to display the grace of perseverance (they) finally testify that the transforming life of Christ has never pulsated within them (*e.g.* Mt. 13:18–23; 24:12; Jn. 8:31ff; Heb. 3:14–19; 1 Jn. 2:19; 2 Jn. 9).[68] The disciples had to learn, like all of us, that Israel was the *type*, but Christ is the superior *antitype* that bears the righteous fruit that satisfies all the expectations of the vinedresser, who is the "Father" (John 15:1b). No one can bear spiritual fruit apart from abiding in the vine of Christ Jesus. Where there is an absence of the fruit of righteousness and persevering faith, there is no spiritual connection and no spiritual life.

The Father—the Vinedresser

Jesus went on to say, "My Father is the vinedresser" (John 15:1b). He is the husbandman who cares for the Vine. It was the Father's tender love for His Son that guarded Him as a child when He "grew up before Him like a tender shoot, and like a root out of parched ground" (Isa. 53:2). But Jesus goes on to explain how the divine husbandman is now occupied with two primary tasks: one, *he must remove branches that bear no fruit*; and two, *he must prune branches that do, so they will bear more fruit*. The distinction between these two kinds of branches was crucial for the disciples' understanding, which Jesus goes on to describe in these words: "Every branch in Me that does not bear fruit, He takes away; and every branch that bears fruit, He prunes it so that it may bear

---

68 D. A. Carson, *The Gospel according to John* (Leicester, England: Inter-Varsity Press; Grand Rapids, Michigan: W.B. Eerdmans, 1991), 515.

more fruit" (John 15:2). These two distinctly different branches symbolize the two kinds of disciples that outwardly profess faith in Christ: the true, fruit-bearing branches who abide in Him versus the false, non-fruit-bearing branches that do not abide in Him.

You may recall how John the Baptist challenged his hearers to "bear fruit in keeping with repentance" (Matt. 3:8), then went on to warn, "Every tree that does not bear good fruit is cut down and thrown into the fire" (v. 10). Judas Iscariot is the most visible example of this. In His parable of the sower (Matt. 13:18–23), Jesus described the *superficial hearers* who attend our churches today: "This is the man who hears the word, and immediately receives it with joy; yet he has no firm root in himself, but is only temporary, and when affliction or persecution arises because of the word, immediately he falls away" (vv. 20–21). He went on to describe *worldly hearers* thus: "The one on whom seed was sown among the thorns, this is the man who hears the word, and the worry of the world, and the deceitfulness of riches choke the word, and it becomes unfruitful" (v. 22). Then finally, in His concluding parable of the wheat and the tares (Matt. 13:24–43), He described how hard it can be to distinguish between true and false disciples, because "both . . . grow together until the harvest," at which time "[He] will say to the reapers, 'First gather up the tares and bind them in bundles to burn them up; but gather the wheat into my barn'" (v. 30).

There have always been and there will always be *false professors* who attach themselves to the church, but not to Christ. This is pandemic in the *institutional church* of Christian liberalism (which is thoroughly apostate), and it makes up the majority of the *cultural church* that dominates the evangelical church today. Plants produce fruit consistent with their nature, according to the genetic information stored in their DNA that provide the instruction used in the development and function of all known live organisms.

The same is true spiritually. Just as plants produce fruit in keeping with their nature, people will do the same. True believers have been made "partakers of the divine nature" (2 Peter 1:4) and will therefore manifest characteristics in keeping with their divine nature. Phony believers will manifest characteristics in keeping with their fallen nature, like the ultra-religious Pharisees of whom Jesus said, "You are of your father the devil, and you want to do the desires of your father . . . . Whenever he speaks a lie, he speaks from his own nature; for he is a liar, and the father of lies" (John 8:44).

Since all true disciples will bear some fruit, Jesus is not referring to Christians who don't bear fruit, but to those who profess Christ in name only, "Christless" Christians who cannot bear fruit in keeping with repentance. Grapes will not grow on thistles! Jesus made this clear when He said, "There is no good tree which produces bad fruit, nor, on the other hand, a bad tree which produces good fruit" (Luke 6:43; cf. Matt. 7:17–20).

Moreover, this does not refer to believers who lose their salvation. Jesus promised He would not forcibly remove any true disciples: "All that the Father gives Me will come to Me, and the one who comes to Me I will certainly not cast out" (John 6:37). It is obvious in Jesus' extended metaphor of the vine and the branches that only dead branches that bear no fruit are thrown away and burned—a judgment motif that extends beyond the Old Testament judgments against Israel, and even beyond the immediate implication of Judas Iscariot, but includes all fruitless branches superficially attached to Jesus through some form of external religious affiliation but not through a vital (living) union by which Christ's life becomes one with those who are in Him (Gal. 2:20; Col. 3:3–4).

Characteristics of Branches that Abide in the Vine

The imagery our Lord provides is a powerful reminder of the mutual indwelling of Christ and His own and the fruitful harvest such an intimate union will produce. There are six prominent characteristics of true branches united to Christ that emerge from His extended metaphor, each providing both comforting assurance and spiritual discernment to those who truly belong to Christ.

FIRST, *all true believers bear spiritual fruit, unlike false disciples who do not and cannot bear spiritual fruit.* As part of this chosen vine, genuine disciples will manifest the fruit in keeping with the source of their life. They will look like Christ! Doing the will of the

Father will be the passion and pattern of their life and they will obey the Word of Christ: "If you continue in My word, then you are truly disciples of Mine" (John 8:31). You don't see any concern for these matters in a false disciple, though he may attend a church, or even be pastor of a church.

Basically, all behavior that is God-honoring will be the fruit of this vine—"fruit in keeping with repentance" (Matt. 3:8)—what Paul called the "fruit of righteousness which comes through Jesus Christ, to the glory and praise of God" (Phil. 1:11). Spiritual fruit includes virtues like the fruit of the Spirit: "love, joy, peace, patience, kindness, goodness, faithfulness, gentleness, self-control" (Gal. 5:22). Every genuine disciple of Christ is a branch attached to the Vine that is Christ, and each branch is a conduit through which the fruit-producing spiritual molecules will flow to produce these magnificent clusters of God-honoring fruit.

SECOND, *not only do true disciples bear fruit, but they abide in Christ's love.* Jesus said, "Just as the Father has loved Me, I have also loved you; abide in My love. If you keep My commandments, you will abide in My love; just as I have kept My Father's commandments and abide in His love" (John 15:9–10). "Abide in my love" is a phrase Jesus uses repeatedly in this metaphor meaning to remain or continue—the obvious result of being united to Christ as Jesus declared, ". . .you in me, and I in you" (John 14:20).

However, it is important not to confuse being *"in Christ"* with *"abiding in Christ."* We are *"in Christ"* permanently as a result of the union effected by God. But we are exhorted to *"abide in Christ,"* meaning we are to remain in fellowship with God in Christ—to have a sustained conscious communion with Him—because sometimes that fellowship is interrupted by sin. So to be "in Christ" is a matter of *grace*; to "abide in Him" is a matter of *responsibility.*

THIRD, *the Father will prune spiritually unproductive branches.* Jesus went on to say, "Every *branch* that bears fruit, He prunes it so that it may bear more fruit. You are already clean because of the word which I have spoken to you" (John 15:2b–3). Like every good husbandman, the Father will cut away those things that restrict our ability to bear fruit, that weaken our spiritual immune system, that inhibit our growth—and Scripture will be His pruning shears. This is why it is so important to be consistently exposed to accurate biblical teaching. The Father is ever vigilant to make us more productive, and He will use the sanctifying truths of His Word (John 17:17) in concert with the circumstances of our life (Rom. 8:28) and His loving discipline (Heb. 12:7–11; *cf.* 1 Cor. 11:32) to make us bear more fruit for His glory and our joy. The Father's "pruning involves cutting away anything that limits righteousness, including the discipline that comes from trials, suffering, and persecution. The knowledge that the Father uses the pain that Christians endure for their ultimate good should eliminate all fear, self-pity, and complaining."[69]

FOURTH, *they will be blessed by answered prayer.* Jesus goes on to make this amazing promise: "If you abide in Me, and My words abide in you, ask whatever you wish, and it will be done for you" (John 15:7). But notice the three conditions for answered prayer. First, *He only answers the prayers of those who abide in Him, who are united to Christ through repentant faith.* Unless it accomplishes His sovereign purposes, God is not obligated to answer the prayers of unbelievers. Second, *prayers must be offered in Jesus' name,* as Jesus stated earlier in chapter 14, "Whatever you ask in My name, that will I do, so that the Father may be glorified in the Son. If you ask Me anything in My name, I will do it" (vv. 13–14). This means that our prayers must be in harmony with God's revealed will in Scripture and His Kingdom purposes. For this reason, Jesus asks us to pray, "Your kingdom come, Your will be done, on earth as it is in heaven" (Matt. 6:10).

Furthermore, we must approach God on the merits of Christ alone, acknowledging our utter dependence upon Him and expressing a sincere desire that God be glorified in His answer, that in all things Christ might have the preeminence.

And finally, *prayers must be offered by those in which Christ's "words abide"*—those who decisively commit themselves to the specific words of Christ, whose lives are controlled by the Word and will of God, not the sinful passions of the flesh and the allurements of the world. It stands to reason that those who abide in Christ and are controlled by His words will ask nothing that is

---

69   John F. MacArthur, *John 12–21: The MacArthur New Testament Commentary* (Chicago, Illinois: Moody Publishers, 1984), 149.

contrary to the will of Christ, and therefore receive whatever they ask.

FIFTH, *they will have the privilege of living lives that glorify God and thus validate the genuineness of their faith.* Jesus said, "My Father is glorified by this, that you bear much fruit, and so prove to be My disciples" (John 15:8). Fruit bearing is the essence of genuine discipleship, the result of abiding in Christ. While it is the Spirit that imparts the principle of holiness within us at regeneration and perfects that good work that He began in us, our new nature cannot operate on its own power. It requires a continued work of sanctification, a constant sustaining and continuous renewing, ". . . for apart from Me you can do nothing" (John 15:5). And it is our Lord's great desire for us to "bear much fruit" so God can receive great glory. Paul stated it this way: ". . . so that you may approve the things that are excellent, in order to be sincere and blameless until the day of Christ; having been filled with the fruit of righteousness which comes through Jesus Christ, to the glory and praise of God" (Phil. 1:10–11).

As we glorify Christ through our obedience—empowered and directed as a result of our living union and communion with Him—we also glorify the Father as He does. The spiritual fruit that adorns the true disciple will reflect the character of Christ to whom we are united, especially when it is bountiful. Like Christ, we glorify the Father through our loving and joyful desire to do His will. As others watch our lives manifest the character of God, they get a small glimpse of who He is, and in this He is glorified and our faith is validated as we show ourselves to be His disciples.

SIXTH, *they will experience the love and joy of intimate fellowship with God.* This would have been so encouraging to the disciples, as it is to all believers, when Jesus said, "Just as the Father has loved Me, I have also loved you; abide in My love. If you keep My commandments, you will abide in My love; just as I have kept My Father's commandments and abide in His love. These things I have spoken to you so that My joy may be in you, and that your joy may be made full" (John 15:9–11). This is the soul-satisfying, Spirit-generated, subjective joy of Christ in the consciousness of the abiding believer. This is what animates a "hope [that] does not disappoint, because the love of God has been poured out within our hearts through the Holy Spirit who was given to us" (Rom. 5:5). Peter described this as "joy inexpressible and full of glory" (1 Peter 1:8), the kind of joy that permeates and controls the life of every obedient believer. Knowing this, Jesus prayed to His Father: "But now I come to You; and these things I speak in the world so that they may have My joy made full in themselves" (John 17:13).

Would that every branch be a live branch that is truly attached *to* the Vine and abides *in* the Vine. Only then can a believer experience and manifest these God-glorifying characteristics which stand in stark contrast to the characteristics of those branches that have never been attached to the Vine through faith.

Characteristics of Branches That Do Not Abide in the Vine

In Jhn 15:2, Jesus gives a strong warning: "Every branch in Me that does not bear fruit, He takes away." He goes on to elaborate upon the fate of a fruitless vine saying, "If anyone does not abide in Me, he is thrown away as a branch and dries up; and they gather them, and cast them into the fire and they are burned" (v. 6). In this context, the phrase *"in Me"* cannot refer to true believers who are united to Christ (because they will always bear fruit and never be taken away). So the Vinedresser (the Father) takes away the branches that have outwardly (superficially) attached themselves to Christ but fail to persevere in the faith. This proves regeneration had never taken place in them, as in the case of Judas Iscariot—the quintessential example of a false (dead) branch.

As I stated earlier, false professors who outwardly resemble true believers will often attach themselves to the church, but not to Christ. However, it is not a man's superficial externals that validate genuine saving faith, but rather it's the Christlike virtues of his heart that produce spiritual fruit. Where the supernatural life in Christ is non-existent, over time the phony Christian will wither away and gradually distance himself or herself from a true New Testament church and break fellowship with true believers. The truth preached will be too hard to hear and impossible to live. Even unwitting hypocrisy is a hard act to maintain. The joy-filled lives and Christ-exalting perseverance of authentic Christians will slowly frustrate pretenders.

Jesus made it clear that such branches will be "gathered up and cast into the fire and burned" (John 15:6). What an unspeakable horror awaits those who refuse to truly embrace Christ in genuine brokenness over sin and in repentant faith. Jesus warns that "at the end of the age the angels will come forth and take out the wicked from among the righteous, and will throw them into the furnace of fire; in that place there will be weeping and gnashing of teeth" (Matt. 13:49–50).

Concluding Thoughts

In this we see the Christian's ambition: *pursuing the prize of Christ-likeness*. While this is never taught in our public schools or universities, and strangely missing in many churches, it is nevertheless essential to the gospel. I trust all Christians will lay hold these truths with all their heart, and with Paul be able to say, "I press on so that I may lay hold of that for which also I was laid hold of by Christ Jesus" (Phil. 3:12). Only then can we enjoy the blessings of our redemption available to us this side of glory; and only then can we be effective in our witness for Christ to a world that hates Him.

8

....

The Christian's Aspiration

Yearning for Heaven

For we know that the whole creation groans and suffers the pains of childbirth together until now. And not only this, but also we ourselves, having the first fruits of the Spirit, even we ourselves groan within ourselves, waiting eagerly for our adoption as sons, the redemption of our body.

Romans 8:18–25

I begin with a true story that will set the stage for the topic of this chapter, *the Christian's Aspiration: Yearning for Heaven*—a passion that is increasing exponentially among the despised saints in pagan America. One of the most remarkable books I have ever read was written by a Scottish divine and biographer, William Garden Blaikie, D.D., LL.D. (1820–1899), Professor of Apologetical and of Pastoral Theology, New College, Edinburgh, Scotland. The title of his work is *The Preachers of Scotland from the Sixth to the Nineteenth Century,*[70] a detailed history of how God empowered fearless servants to bring the gospel to the wild barbarians of Scotland, and how that gospel saved and radically changed them. As I was transported to another time and another place, I was deeply impacted by the great mystery of godliness at work in the early days of Scotland when

> . . . missionaries, with tearful eye and trembling lip, told them of the manger of Bethlehem and the cross of Calvary. What else could have dispossessed the old gods from their hearts at a stroke, spite of all they had learned from their fathers? What else could have turned these shaggy men and women, hardly less wild-looking than the cattle of their mountains, into devout and earnest followers of a crucified Jew?[71]

With vivid language and biblical theology—combined with first-source historical accounts from eyewitness testimonies, journals, and some recorded sermons—Blaikie took me on an unforgettable journey to witness the power of God at work in a pagan land. From the earliest days when Roman soldiers in the invading army were "moved by the love of Christ," and "followed it to cast the seed of the Gospel into the furrows of war,"[72] through the great preachers of the Reformation and Covenanting Period of Scotland, his recounting of history caused me to stand in reverential awe as I beheld the agencies of divine providence at work in accomplishing the sovereign purposes of God.

---

70   William Garden Blaikie, *The Preachers of Scotland from the Sixth to the Nineteenth Century* (T. & T. Clark, Edinburgh, 1888; reproduced by BiblioLife, LLC), 1.

71   Ibid., 22–23.

72   Ibid., 14.

The annals of Scottish religious history repeatedly demonstrated how the power of sound doctrine (decidedly Calvinistic) would prevail over the church's tendency toward compromise, especially in those seasons when it embraced the "doctrines of Pelagianism and Arminianism" that "ultimately developed into deism and indifferentism"[73] like we witness in America today. But his chronicles of the persecuted field-preachers that resulted from the edicts of King Charles II of England were particularly moving to me, especially given the escalating hostilities toward authentic Christians in our country at the hands of *secular government* and *false religious systems* that conspire together to thwart the purposes of God.

Field-Preachers—Men of Uncommon Valor

During the dreadful years of persecution between 1663 and 1688, young clergymen who championed Presbyterian church polity and a robust Reformed soteriology were driven from their charges, and under the "threat of fine and imprisonment, of torture or of death"[74] were restricted from preaching the only gospel that can save people. With no way of earning a living, and with orders from the king to inflict heavy fines, imprisonment, and even torture leading to death upon anyone who helped them, "the preacher, with a great price on his head, had no certain dwelling-place, and where there was no friendly cottage to shelter him, had to wander about in wild lonely places, sleeping in woods and caves, often cold and wet and hungry; racked by rheumatism or prostrated by dysentery, glad if he could succeed in keeping his pocket-Bible dry."[75]

These great soldiers of the cross were affectionately called, "Field-Preachers"—men of uncommon valor. With somber colors Blaikie painted the tragedies and triumphs of those days on a dark canvas of satanic oppression. He writes,

If ever circumstances compelled the Lord's servants to preach "as dying men to dying men," it was then. Neither

73 Ibid., 150.
74 Ibid., 156.
75 Ibid., 157.

preacher nor hearer could ever be sure that the dragoons would not burst on them before the sermon was ended, or that before nightfall their life-blood would not be staining the ground. . . . Preachers seemed at times to feel the bloody rope round their neck, or the bullet in their brain; the word came from their hearts and went to the hearts of their hearers, and stuck there for their conversion, confirmation, and comfort. Persecution, like the deathbed, has a wonderful sifting power. It tears away all disguises, shams, falsehoods, and formalities; it compels men to look the stern realities of life and death right in the face, it sweeps away the refuges of lies, and leaves only those truths to cling to which will sustain them in the agony of conflict.[76]

Despite the satanic onslaught of persecution designed to terrorize both the field-preachers and those who would hear them with the threat of imprisonment and death—often a slow and agonizing death—these men proclaimed the unsearchable riches of Christ with fervent boldness. Their sermons thundered across the moors and mountain-recesses of the northern third of Britain, often to massive crowds who were hungry for the great saving, liberating, and transforming truths of the gospel—a phenomenon we see developing in our country as many are searching for real answers to life's problems in a culture that has none.

Richard Cameron

One such field-preacher was a young man named Richard Cameron (c. 1648 – 22 July 1680); a man who refused to submit to the Crown's High Church Anglican form of church governance (episcopacy) that sought to control the Church of Scotland through their appointed (apostate) bishops and demanded that the king be considered the head of the church (rather than Christ). Refusing to submit to such an unbiblical ecclesiology with its associated heresies, Cameron became a leader of the militant Presbyterians known as the Covenanters.

A born preacher with no formal theological training apart from

---

76   Ibid., 157–58.

what he received from other field-preachers, he was a mighty and fearless preacher in the spirit of the apostles. In his book, *The Scottish Covenanters: 1638–88,* James Dodds (1813–1874) paints a beautiful picture of the Spirit-empowered revivals that marked those days—a season when thousands of saints and sinners met in the wilderness to worship God by hearing Cameron preach the gospel while other men stood guard in the distance. Here's a description of such a scene:

> Picture to yourselves this noble and majestic youth, with blooming countenance and eagle eye, standing on some huge rock uplifted in the wilderness. Ten thousand people are grouped around him: the aged, with the women and children, seated near this pulpit of nature's handiwork; the men of middle age and the stalwart youths of the surrounding hamlets composing the outer circle, many of them with their hands on their swords, or their trusty guns slung by their side; and on each neighbouring height may be seen the solitary figure of the watchman, intently gazing in all directions for the approach of the troopers who are now kept garrisoned in every district, and who night and day are on the prowl to catch some poor outlawed Covenanter, or surprise some conventicle in the depths of the hills. It is a Sabbath in May. The great wild moor stretches out to a kind of infinity, blending at last with the serene blue sky. How sublime and peaceful the moment! Even in this age of violence and oppression—of the dungeon, the rack, and the scaffold, and murder in cold blood in the fields. Heaven smiles on the "remnant." All is hushed and reverent in attention. The word is precious. . . . The psalm has been sung, and the echoes of the myriad voices have died on the moorland breeze. The prayer has been offered, the earnest wrestlings with Heaven of men who before sunset may themselves be an offering for their religion. The preacher rises. He eyes for a moment in silence that vast multitude, gathered from all parts of the West. Always serious, always inspired with elevated feeling, there is in his manner more than the usual solemnity. . . . Yes, he knows that his days are numbered;

and but a few more suns the heather sod shall be his bed of death. A strange, almost unearthly sympathy is visible, stirring those assembled thousands to the very depths of their being. Rousing himself from the reverie which had passed over him, the preacher announces his text—"Ye will not come to me that ye might have life."[77]

Young Cameron knew how to tap into the resources that were his because of his union with Christ. He, along with the beleaguered saints of Scotland, knew what it was to yearn for heaven. Together they lived out the inspired words of the apostle Paul:

Therefore if you have been raised up with Christ, keep seeking the things above, where Christ is, seated at the right hand of God. Set your mind on the things above, not on the things that are on earth. For you have died and your life is hidden with Christ in God. When Christ, who is our life, is revealed, then you also will be revealed with Him in glory. (Col. 3:1–4)

The young field-preacher knew what it was to "Suffer hardship . . . as a good soldier of Christ Jesus" (2 Tim. 2:1, 3). And suffer he did.

On 22 July, government dragoons killed Cameron at Airds Moss near Cumnock. There they mutilated his body by severing his hands and head from it. Then, in perhaps a more heinous act of barbaric cruelty, they took his head and hands to Edinburgh to show to his father who was incarcerated there for the same crimes. It is hard to imagine a more macabre scene, or fathom a more satanic hatred capable of evoking such evil in the hearts of men. When the father was asked if he recognized the hands and head he responded, "I know them. I know them. They are my son's, my own dear son's. It is the Lord. Good is the will of the Lord, who cannot wrong me or mine, but has made goodness and mercy to follow us all our days."[78] His son's head was then placed

---

77 James Dodds, *The Scottish Covenanters, 1638–88* (Edmonston and Douglas, 1860, Second Edition) 268–79. (See, https://archive.org/details/fiftyyearsstrugg00dodd/page/n7.)

78 Jock Purves, *Fair Sunshine: Character Studies of the Scottish Covenanters* (Carlisle, Pennsylvania: Banner of Truth Trust, 2003), 58.

upon a pole and paraded through the streets of Edinburgh. His hands and his head were finally affixed to the Nether-Bow Gate for public display.[79]

Elusive Spiritual Strength

When considering the violent opposition to the truth that has marked not only the history of Scotland, but countless other countries, any reasonable man must admit that something super-natural is at work. It is something so sinister, so evil, so powerful, that it can only be described as Satanic—like what we see happening in America. Truly we "wrestle not against flesh and blood, but against the rulers, against the powers, against the world forces of this darkness, against the spiritual forces of wickedness in the heavenly places" (Eph. 6:12) and this requires every Christian to "be strong in the Lord, and in the strength of His might" (Eph. 6:10), like Richard Cameron and thousands of others like him through the course of redemptive history.

Jesus warned us that the world would always hate those who belong to Him "because you are not of the world, but I chose you out of the world, therefore the world hates you" (John 15:19). From the days of the Old Testament prophets through the New Testament era of Christ and the apostles, divinely appointed men who have proclaimed the truths of God's revelation have been violently opposed, imprisoned, tortured, and killed—our sinless Savior being the supreme example. *Foxe's Book of Martyrs* provides numerous examples of men and women during the time of the Reformation who took a stand against the religious abuses that had taken over the church. Untold numbers of godly men and women who embraced the true gospel were so hated by the forces of evil that they were forced to pay for their faith with their very lives.

This has been, and will continue to be, the history of the church until Christ returns. The historical hatred of New Testament Christianity (unlike the numerous counterfeits that have always existed) is nothing strange to those who belong to Christ. They understand their citizenship is in heaven (Phil. 3:20)

---

79 William Garden Blaikie, *The Preachers of Scotland from the Sixth to the Nineteenth Century* (T. & T. Clark, Edinburgh, 1888; reproduced by BiblioLife, LLC), 177.

and they are therefore content to be "aliens and strangers" (1 Peter 2:11) in a world of which they have no part (John 15:19). But this doesn't make it any easier when it comes to doing battle with sin—whether their sin or the sin of others. Although we know "that the sufferings of this present time are not worthy to be compared with the glory that is to be revealed to us" (Rom. 8:18), we still "groan within ourselves, waiting eagerly for our adoption as sons, the redemption of our body" (Rom. 8:23) when in our glorification we finally and fully enter into the ineffable splendor of our inheritance. Even our Lord was "despised and forsaken of men, a man of sorrows and acquainted with grief" (Isa. 53:3) and was so overcome by the prospect of the cross that an angel was sent to strengthen him in the garden of Gethsemane (Luke 22:43).

Though the agonies of Christ were infinitely greater than anything we would ever even imagine much less endure, we are prone to debilitating fear, discouragement, and spiritual weakness. But knowing how to rise above them—especially in the face of persecution—is elusive for most people. Unfortunately, far too often men and women who have demonstrated remarkable strength of character and resolute faith in the midst of some great trial are considered to be the recipients of supernatural resources unavailable to the average Christian and therefore unattainable to most. But such is not the case. Every believer united to Christ in saving faith possesses all that is His—what Paul described as "the surpassing greatness of His power toward us who believe . . . in accordance with the working of the strength of His might which He brought about in Christ" (Eph. 1:19–20).

The apostle Paul exhibited this throughout his life and ministry, as discussed earlier in this book. But we see the same strength of character and resolute faith in the apostle Peter, after the Holy Spirit came upon him at Pentecost. And we see this manifested in his inspired epistles to the scattered and persecuted saints of the first century. I pray that by God's grace and the power of His Spirit a cursory overview of his words will bring a special measure of encouragement to any reader who may be struggling with his or her faith amidst the dangers developing so rapidly in America.

Persecution in the First-Century Church

What the suffering saints of the nascent church endured at the hands of Rome makes all we're experiencing in America pale in comparison. Nevertheless, the truths God used to bless them are equally beneficial to all believers in all circumstances. Because of His great love for His own people, God brought great comfort to them through His servant Peter. And to think Peter wrote his epistles with the full knowledge that his life would ultimately end on a Roman cross (as Jesus promised in John 21). He wrote 1 Peter around AD 65 and 2 Peter just before he was crucified in AD 67 or 68. How would you like to serve Christ all your life knowing this would be your manner of death? Tradition says Peter was forced to watch his wife be crucified before it was his turn, and all the while he kept saying to her, "Remember the Lord." Then when it was his turn, he asked to be crucified upside down, considering himself unworthy to be crucified in the same manner as his Savior, the Lord Jesus Christ.

Non-Christians of the first century, like the unregenerate of our day, resented the message of the gospel and despised Christians. You might say it was "politically correct" to do so. Jews and Gentiles resented how they disrupted families with their newfound faith, which they considered to be an arrogant religion that demeaned others. Being called a depraved sinner, alienated from God and destined to eternal wrath, is not a message anyone wants to hear. Being warned of their eternal doom if they refused to abandon their pagan beliefs and trust in Jesus Christ didn't go over any better in the first century than it does in the twenty-first century, except for those who are given the gift of faith (Eph. 2:8–9). Isn't it fascinating how Christians today are called "haters" and "bigots" who discriminate against others? Of course there was already plenty of hatred to go around between Jews and Gentiles; and to make things worse, the Gentiles considered Christianity to be an extremist faction of Judaism.

First-century Rome also had its version of "Fake News" just like we have in America. The spin machine called Christians *cannibals* because they ate the flesh and drank the blood of Christ during the Lord's Supper. They were called *immoral* because they loved to fellowship with one another and they greeted one another with a holy kiss. They were also designated as *insurrectionists* because they bowed only to Jesus as King and declared citizenship of another kingdom.

By the time Peter wrote his first epistle to the saints scattered abroad in Asia Minor (modern-day Turkey), the animosity against Christians was trending toward genocide. Satan's emissary, the barbaric and insane Emperor Nero, used this mounting hatred to his political advantage. Because of his insatiable appetite to glorify himself, he set Rome on fire in AD 64 and blamed it on the Christians.

Roman historian Tacitus records how Christians were blamed not only for the burning of Rome, but also for their hatred of the human race. He described how they were subjected to fiendish tortures and how it was great sport for Nero to sew bloody animal hides on them and feed them to wild animals. Thousands were crucified and many were dipped in wax and burned alive to illuminate his gardens as he wildly drove his chariot through his private hippodrome.[80]

It was in this season of Christian persecution that both Peter and Paul and many others were martyred, and it was on the precipice of this inconceivable era of suffering that they penned their epistles. As things worsened, by the fourth century the Emperor Diocletian tried to eradicate Christianity—until Constantine came to its rescue in AD 313. One writer described those first 300 years of persecution this way:

> Horror spread everywhere through the congregations; and the number of lapsi (the ones who renounced their faith when threatened) . . . was enormous. There was no lack, however, of such as remained firm, and suffered martyrdom rather than yielding; and, as the persecution grew wider and more intense, the enthusiasm of the Christians and their power of resistance grew stronger and stronger.[81]

But soon after Constantine's deliverance, during the Middle

---

80 https://www.livius.org/sources/content/tacitus/tacitus-on-the-christians/
81 *Schaff-Herzog Encyclopedia of Religious Knowledge, vol. 1* (New York: Funk & Wagnalls, Publishers, 1882), 620

Ages, the church became so deceived by false teachers that it lost all discernment and gradually morphed into the Roman Catholic Church, which replaced Imperial Rome. With the political power of the papacy, they tried to eliminate the gospel completely and, in the process, tortured and killed millions during the Inquisition. Millions more from that day to the present have been killed by Jesuits and their alliance with Communist regimes.

Christian Persecution Today around the World

Today the persecution continues. To be a Christian in many countries is to risk losing your possessions, your family, and even your life. According to *Open Doors*—a community of Christians who come together to support persecuted believers in more than fifty countries—the following data demonstrates how widespread Christian persecution really is (data acquired from October 31, 2017 to November 1, 2018):

- 245 Million: In the top 50 World Watch List [WWL] countries alone, 245 million Christians in the world experience high levels of persecution for their choice to follow Christ.
- 1 in 9: Christians worldwide experience high levels of persecution.
- 14%: The rise in the number of Christians in the top 50 countries on the 2019 World Watch List (WWL) who experience high levels of persecution. (From the 2018 reporting period to 2019's.)
- 4,136: Christians killed for faith-related reasons in the top 50 WWL countries.
- 2,625: Christians detained without trial, arrested, sentenced and imprisoned in the top 50 WWL countries.
- 1,266: churches or Christian buildings attacked in the top 50 WWL countries.
- 7 out of 9: In seven of the countries in the World Watch List's top 10, the primary cause of persecution is Islamic oppression.
- 11: countries scoring in the "extreme" level for their persecution of Christians. Five years ago, North Korea was the

only one.

* 18: Consecutive years North Korea has ranked No. 1 as the world's most dangerous place for Christians.[82]

Whenever I've had the opportunity of teaching in third-world countries where life is difficult, or in countries like Siberia where Christians continue to live under oppressive anti-Christian rule, the topic of heaven is always the most popular. The hearts of my listeners have no desire for the paltry pleasures of earth, nor do they have material treasures to take pleasure in. Yet their joy is contagious, for they have stored up for themselves "treasures in heaven . . . for where your treasure is, there your heart will be also" (Matt. 6:20). They know what it is to yearn for heaven, the deepest longing of the redeemed expressed by the psalmist who said, "As the deer pants for the water brooks, so my soul pants for You, O God" (Ps. 42:1). Persecution animates this longing all the more, causing Christians to feel the reality of being "strangers and exiles on the earth" (Heb. 11:13) more acutely.

While America's hatred of biblical Christianity is very real, it has not escalated to the same level of severity as we witness in other parts of the world, although it is growing; and the more the neo-Marxists take control, the more rapidly it will develop—so, all the more reason for Christians to have the kind of biblical perspective the Spirit of God has given to us. A brief overview of just a few passages in 1 Peter reveals the kinds of doctrinal priorities the persecuted saints should possess and call to mind in days of adversity—truths that fanned the flames of their longing for glory all the more. I will merely touch upon four key principles to remember.

What We Must Remember in Times of Persecution

FIRST, *Remember God has chosen us according to His uninfluenced sovereign love.*

This is where Peter begins, as must we. He reminded them that they were "chosen according to the foreknowledge of God the Fa-

---

82 https://www.opendoorsusa.org/christian-persecution/stories/christian-persecution-by-the-numbers/

ther, by the sanctifying work of the Spirit, to obey Jesus Christ and be sprinkled with His blood" (1 Peter 1:1-2). Can there be any greater consolation in sorrow than to know that God set His love upon us and chose us by His grace alone? Indeed, "He chose us in Him [Christ] before the foundation of the world, that we would be holy and blameless before Him. In love He predestined us to adoption as sons through Jesus Christ to Himself, according to the kind intention of His will, to the praise of the glory of His grace, which He freely bestowed on us in the Beloved" (Eph. 1:4-6).

We would all do well to remember this foundational truth when the world casts us away and we feel the crushing blows of being "aliens and strangers" (1 Peter 2:11) in this world. Remember this the next time your friends or coworkers mock your convictions or your employer shows you the door. Remember to whom you belong—forever! Again in 1 Peter 2:9, Peter reiterates the inestimable privilege and purpose of being among God's elect, "But you are a chosen race, a royal priesthood, a holy nation, a people for God's own possession, so that you may proclaim the excellencies of Him who has called you out of darkness into His marvelous light." Given His sovereign choice of us, we have no reason to doubt His good purposes for us. Nor have we any reason to fear that anything might separate us from His love. To this end Paul writes:

What then shall we say to these things? If God is for us, who is against us? He who did not spare His own Son, but delivered Him over for us all, how will He not also with Him freely give us all things? Who will bring a charge against God's elect? God is the one who justifies; who is the one who condemns? Christ Jesus is He who died, yes, rather who was raised, who is at the right hand of God, who also intercedes for us. Who will separate us from the love of Christ? Will tribulation, or distress, or persecution, or famine, or nakedness, or peril, or sword? Just as it is written, "For Your sake we are being put to death all day long; We were considered as sheep to be slaughtered." But in all these things we overwhelmingly conquer through Him who loved us. For I am convinced that neither death, nor life, nor angels, nor principalities, nor

things present, nor things to come, nor powers, nor height, nor depth, nor any other created thing, will be able to separate us from the love of God, which is in Christ Jesus our Lord.
(Rom. 8:31–39)

SECOND, *Remember God is the Source of our hope.*

We see this in Peter's doxology, "Blessed be the God and Father of our Lord Jesus Christ, who according to His great mercy has caused us to be born again to a living hope through the resurrection of Jesus Christ from the dead" (1 Peter 1:3). What an amazing thought! He is both our Creator and spiritual Father. "In the exercise of His will He brought us forth [the verb can be rendered "gives birth"] by the word of truth, so that we might be, as it were, the first fruits among His creatures" (James 1:8). Those "who are being led by the Spirit of God . . . are sons of God . . . [and] have received a spirit of adoption as sons by which we cry out, "Abba! Father!" (Rom. 8:14–15), and for this reason we are "heirs of God and fellow heirs with Christ" (Rom. 8:17).

Think how magnificent this is: *He saves us from sin, raises us from spiritual death to life, adopts us as his own, and makes us His spiritual children*: "But as many as received Him, to them He gave the right to become children of God, even to those who believe in His name" (John 1:12). And because we are His children, He has promised to care for us and meet all our needs—even during a pandemic or when our biblical convictions are outlawed and we lose our jobs because we refuse to bow to the false gods of our culture.

More frequently than ever before in my ministry, I'm being called upon to comfort faithful believers who have suffered great financial loss because the PC police exposed some biblical conviction that was at odds with theirs. I'm increasingly bringing beleaguered saints to 1 Peter, and other passages filled with promise, including the words of Jesus who said,

Do not worry then, saying, "What will we eat?" or "What will we drink?" or "What will we wear for clothing?" For the Gentiles eagerly seek all these things; for your heavenly Father knows that you need all these things. But seek first His kingdom and His righteousness, and all these things will be added to you. So do not worry about tomorrow; for tomorrow will care for itself. Each day has enough trouble of its own. (Matt. 6:31–34)

THIRD, *Remember God is the Protector of our hope.*

This would have been profoundly encouraging to those believers who had lost loved ones because of their faithfulness to Christ and were facing the very real possibility of death themselves. Peter wanted them to remember that they have "an inheritance which is imperishable and undefiled and will not fade away, reserved in heaven for you, who are protected by the power of God through faith for a salvation ready to be revealed in the last time" (1 Peter 1:4–5).

What a magnificent and mysterious promise! We hope "to obtain an inheritance" (1 Peter 1:4), which denotes property and possession. Paul speaks of this in Colossians 1:12 where he writes, "Give thanks to the Father, who has qualified us to share in the inheritance of the saints in light." Here Paul reaches back into the Old Testament by alluding to the specific land allotments given to the Israelites when they entered into Canaan to possess it (Num. 26, 33). The term "inheritance" (*klēronomia*) is literally, "a portion or share of an allotment." This means the Father "has qualified [authorized] us [according to His grace] to share in the inheritance of the saints in light" ("light" being a synonym for the kingdom of God/heaven), and in this glorious kingdom each believer will be given a specific portion of the total divine inheritance. While we cannot fathom all that this will include, we know it will be ineffably glorious.

No doubt it will include specific possessions and privileges for us to enjoy and serve God in ways beyond our ability to comprehend. Paul refers to this again in Colossians 3:24: "...know that from the Lord you will receive the reward of the inheritance"; and again in Ephesians 1:11: "[Because of our Father's great mercy] we have obtained an inheritance"; as does the writer of Hebrews in 9:15, mentioning how ". . . those who have been called may receive the promise of the eternal inheritance."

But to know that God is the One who protects the very inheritance that He has given us is truly mind-boggling. By declaring that the believer's inheritance is "reserved in heaven" he's underscoring not only its permanence, but also its current existence. The term "reserved" (*tetērēmenēn*) carries the idea of being "kept" or "guarded". It is a perfect passive participle, denoting God as the One who reserves (guards) the inheritance that is already in existence in heaven and awaits those "who are protected by the power of God through faith for a salvation ready to be revealed in the last time" (1 Peter 1:5).

What a glorious thought to know that God has freely given us an inheritance that He personally protects by His omnipotent power until it is ready to be revealed to us "in the last time" (1 Peter 1:5), a reference to the new heaven and new earth for which we yearn. We are given a sneak peek of what this will include in Revelation 21 and also in 22:1–5:

> Then he showed me a river of the water of life, clear as crystal, coming from the throne of God and of the Lamb, in the middle of its street. On either side of the river was the tree of life, bearing twelve kinds of fruit, yielding its fruit every month; and the leaves of the tree were for the healing of the nations. There will no longer be any curse; and the throne of God and of the Lamb will be in it, and His bond-servants will serve Him; they will see His face, and His name will be on their foreheads. And there will no longer be any night; and they will not have need of the light of a lamp nor the light of the sun, because the Lord God will illumine them; and they will reign forever and ever.

FOURTH, *Remember God is the Refiner of our hope.*

We see this in Peter's encouraging words in verses 6–9. This is a passage many saints have committed to memory because of the clarity and conviction in brings to those who find themselves in some great storm of sorrow that seems to be swallowing them up:

In this you greatly rejoice, even though now for a little while, if necessary, you have been distressed by various trials, so that the proof of your faith, being more precious than gold which is perishable, even though tested by fire, may be found to result in praise and glory and honor at the revelation of Jesus Christ; and though you have not seen Him, you love Him, and though you do not see Him now, but believe in Him, you greatly rejoice with joy inexpressible and full of glory, obtaining as the outcome of your faith the salvation of your souls.
(1 Peter 1:6–9)

Whenever I read this passage, I'm reminded of a little hymn written by Jim Hill that I have sung many times with the precious saints in my church family at the close of an outdoor baptismal service at Sycamore Creek. Perhaps you have sung it as well:

What a day that will be,
When my Jesus I shall see,
And I look upon His face,
The One who saved me by His grace;
When He takes me by the hand,
And leads me through the Promised Land,
What a day, glorious day that will be.

There'll be no sorrow there,
No more burdens to bear,
No more sickness, no more pain,
No more parting over there;
But forever I will be,
With the One who died for me,
What a day, glorious day that will be.

What a day that will be,
When my Jesus I shall see,
When I look upon His face,
The One who saved me by His grace;

When He takes me by the hand,
And leads me through that Promised Land,
What a day, glorious day that will be.

To be sure, "In this you greatly rejoice, even though now for a little while, if necessary, you have been distressed by various trials, so that the proof of your faith, being more precious than gold which is perishable, even though tested by fire, may be found to result in praise and glory and honor at the revelation of Jesus Christ" (1 Peter 1:6–7). Here we are all comforted knowing that God is indeed the *Refiner of our hope.*

We must also remember, however, that the justified saint is the one who exults *on account of* his tribulations (Rom. 5:3) because he understands the law of divine providence is weaving an infinitely glorious tapestry in which he is privileged to be a small part. With Shadrach, Meshach, and Abed-nego—who experienced the presence of the living Christ in the fires of Nebuchadnezzar—he can say, "there is no other God who is able to deliver in this way!" (Dan. 3:29). What an amazing thing it is to experience the presence of Almighty God while in some unexpected crucible of His grace. This was also at the heart of Peter's encouragement to the suffering saints of his day when he wrote, "Beloved, do not be surprised at the fiery ordeal among you, which comes upon you for your testing, as though some strange thing were happening to you" (1 Peter 4:12). In other words, "Don't act as if it were some accident that caught God by surprise, that somehow this was outside the purview of His will. Don't respond that way."

He went on to say, "But to the degree that you share the sufferings of Christ, keep on rejoicing, so that also at the revelation of His glory, you may rejoice with exultation. If you are reviled for the name of Christ, you are blessed, because the Spirit of glory and of God rests upon you" (1 Peter 4:13–14). Then, later, he gives this exhortation with the promise: "Humble yourselves, therefore, under the mighty hand of God, that He may exalt you at the proper time, casting all your anxiety upon Him, because He cares for you" (1 Peter 5:6–7).

Two Events We Eagerly Await

Shifting from the encouraging words of Peter to those of Paul, we are also reminded of the new possibilities that open up during severe hardships. Paul exhorts us to "exult in hope of the glory of God" (see Rom. 5:2b–5). As we examine this phrase in light of other passages, we see there are two events that await us, events every justified saint will someday experience. First, *we are going to experience an unrestricted, personal fellowship with the Triune God.* Second, *we are going to experience a personal transformation into the glory of Christ.* This is why we "exult in hope of the glory of God." Knowing the certain fulfillment of these promises should further animate our heart to praise and greatly impact how we live (1 John 3:3). They should also cause us to yearn for heaven all the more.

THINK FIRST of having an *unrestricted, personal fellowship with the Triune God.* Can you imagine what it will be like when we see God face to face? Yet this will be one of the blessings that belong to the redeemed. Jesus promised, "Blessed are the pure in heart, for they shall see God" (Matt. 5:8). But, how can we have purity of heart since we already know that it doesn't come from anything we can do? It's *the result of justification.* Only the justified will be able to experience unrestricted, personal fellowship with the Triune God.

Knowing that we will finally see the Savior we love face to face is a promise that has animated the hearts of the redeemed with inexpressible joy for millennia. How many times have I tearfully said to the Lord in prayer, "Oh, how I wish I could see You now!" No doubt you have done the same. This was certainly the heart of the blind nineteenth-century hymn writer, Fanny Crosby, who expressed her longing to see Christ in the words of her hymn, "My Savior First of All." There she wrote:

> *When my life work is ended, and I cross the swelling tide,*
> *When the bright and glorious morning I shall see,*
> *I shall know my Redeemer when I reach the other side,*
> *And His smile will be the first to welcome me. . .*

Thru the gates to the city in a robe of spotless white,
He will lead me where no tears will ever fall;
In the glad song of ages I shall mingle with delight,
But I long to meet my Savior first of all.

Paul helps us understand what it means to see God when he writes, "For now we see in a mirror dimly, but then face to face; now I know in part, but then I shall know fully just as I also have been fully known" (1 Cor. 13:12). The Greek word "know" in this text means to accurately and intimately perceive and understand. Not only will we see the glory of God when we see Him face to face, but we will have the same kind of intimate understanding of His person and His character, likened to the knowledge that He has of us. Paul expresses this when he says, ". . . then I shall know fully just as I also have been fully known" (1 Cor. 13:12).

Staggering, isn't it? Thrilling; motivating! No wonder Paul says, "I want you to rejoice in hope of the glory of God." It's as if he's saying, "I want you to be consumed with sheer jubilation when you reflect upon the immovable standing that is yours in grace that guarantees all of this will one day come to fruition when faith will be turned to sight." Therefore, "Exult in hope of the glory of God" (Rom. 5:2).

Bear in mind that Paul had already experienced some measure of this when he penned these words to the saints in Rome. He knew exactly what awaited them. In fact, he gave us a glimpse of this intimate fellowship when he described to the Corinthians his own supernatural experience:

> I know a man in Christ who fourteen years ago—whether in the body I do not know, or out of the body I do not know, God knows—such a man was caught up to the third heaven. And I know how such a man—whether in the body or apart from the body I do not know, God knows—was caught up into Paradise, and heard inexpressible words, which a man is not permitted to speak.
> (2 Cor. 12:2–4)

When we look at other writings of Paul, we get some sense of what he saw and experienced. These things were so unspeakably glorious that all he could say was simply to *exult in hope of the glory of God!* It's as though he smiles while shaking his head in dismay and says, "I can't even begin to describe this to you, but trust me: the glory of God exceeds the limits of anything you can imagine!"

In 2 Corinthians 12:5, Paul says something else that is very interesting about his encounter with God. He says, "On behalf of such a man will I boast; but on my own behalf I will not boast, except in regard to my weaknesses." The Greek word for "boast" is the same term used in Romans 5:2 where he says we "exult ["boast" or "rejoice"] in hope of the glory of God." Paul is essentially saying, "I jump for joy in sheer jubilation when I reflect upon my confident hope of our future bliss—that which I saw and heard." This should be the response of every saint. Like Paul, we also "exult in hope of the glory of God" because one day we will experience unrestricted personal fellowship with the Triune God who has revealed Himself in Scripture and in the person and work of His beloved Son, our Savior, the Lord Jesus Christ!

One day we will see something so astounding, so breathtakingly transcendent, that, by comparison, "the sufferings of this present time are not worthy to be compared with the glory that is to be revealed to us" (Rom. 8:18). This will not only include the astounding splendors of heaven, but, most importantly, it will comprehend an unrestricted personal fellowship with the Lover our soul. We will be able to know God in ways exceedingly beyond our awareness of Him now.

BUT SECONDLY, when considering what it means to "exult in hope of the glory of God," Paul wants us to contemplate the promise of *a personal transformation into the glory of Christ.*

Consider two texts of Scripture. First, in Hebrews 1:3, the writer speaks of Jesus as being, "the radiance of [God's] glory and the exact representation of His nature." And Paul says, "For whom He foreknew, He also predestined to become conformed to the image of His Son" (Rom. 8:29). Putting these Scriptures together, we see that God has predestined believers to share in the likeness of God in terms of the glory of His character (*cf.* 1 Cor. 15:50, 53). Although we will have a different makeup with respect to how we are constructed, our external appearance will be like His.

The Father is not going to present to His Son an ugly bride. Instead, as we read in Ephesians 5:27, God desires to "present to Himself the church in all her glory, having no spot or wrinkle or any such thing; but that she should be holy and blameless." In fact, we have been "prepared beforehand for glory" (Rom. 9:23).

In 2 Corinthians 3:18, Paul adds this fascinating statement: "But we all being transformed into the same image from glory to glory, just as from the Lord, the Spirit." Think about this. Wherever you are right now at this very moment you are *being transformed*. Grammatically, the phrase "being transformed" translates a present passive participle. It is from the verb *metamorphoo*, from which we get our word "metamorphosis." Notice, too, that this transformation happens in stages. We continue to do this as we behold Him—a continual and progressive process. Our sanctification is empowered by the indwelling Spirit of God, who alone can gradually conform us into the image of the Lord Jesus Christ.

This "being transformed" is similar to what Paul says in Romans 12:2, where he uses the same verb. There is a metamorphosis that occurs by the renewing of our mind. That is why Paul says that we are ascending from "glory to glory" until one day we are like Him (2 Cor. 3:18). As we see God and as we see the glory of Christ through Scripture, we gradually begin to manifest on the outside who we truly are on the inside. Paul described it this way:

> For our citizenship is in heaven, from which also we eagerly wait for a Savior, the Lord Jesus Christ; who will transform the body of our humble state into conformity with the body of His glory, by the exertion of the power that He has even to subject all things to Himself.
> (Phil. 3:20–21)

This subjection will undoubtedly include the creation of new laws of physics. Don't you long for that resurrected body? Oh, to be like Christ! As we study this in Scripture, it is more than simply a "new and improved" version of ourselves. No, it is a *totally new and completely recreated body*. In 1 Corinthians 15, Paul tells how we are going to be raised imperishable, in power.

In death, what is sown in dishonor and weakness will be raised in glory and power. Like His own glorious body, we will be given a spiritual body beyond anything we can comprehend—one suited for eternal life beyond the limits of time and space in which we exist today.

The Motivating Force of Anticipated Glory

In 2 Corinthians 4:17–18, Paul anticipates this coming glory and his words help us to put our present sufferings into perspective. He says, "For momentary, light affliction is producing for us an eternal weight of glory far beyond all comparison." In short, future glory outweighs anything that we can experience in terms of suffering in this life. He goes on to say that "we look not at the things which are seen, but at the things which are not seen; for the things which are seen are temporal, but the things which are not seen are eternal."

This should change our perspective. True endurance in the faith and overcoming the many obstacles we encounter in this fallen world requires looking beyond the temporal and the physical. Instead, we must gaze into the eternal through eyes of faith. Admittedly, we don't see completely or clearly right now, but we have a certain hope that one day we will see and experience all that He has granted us in the fullness of divinely wrought perfection.

It is not uncommon to experience the joys of Eden one minute and the sorrows of Gethsemane the next. But ultimately we have the certain hope of seeing Christ in all His glory. "We know that when He appears, we will be like Him, because we will see Him just as He is" (1 John 3:2). Theologians have described this as the *Beatific Vision*—that moment when we will feast our souls on the visible presence of Christ and enjoy the infinite beauty and love of God forever. That day, we will see God and "stand in His presence blameless with great joy" (Jude 24). That is the instant when, for the first time, we will experience the unhindered, perfected, fullness of Triune love. Can there be any greater promise to bring joy to our soul?

Oh, that we would rejoice in this blessed hope! There is a

process of sanctification presently at work that will culminate in these glorious truths. That is why we can sing with Charles Wesley:

> *Changed from glory into glory,*
> *'Til in heaven we take our place,*
> *'Til we cast our crowns before thee,*
> *Lost in wonder, love and praise.*

Concluding Thoughts

Although most people believe in some kind of heaven (though most do not believe in hell), few will ever enter in. Jesus made this clear when He said, "Not everyone who says to Me, 'Lord, Lord,' will enter the kingdom of heaven, but he who does the will of My Father who is in heaven will enter" (Matt. 7:21). And it is the will of the Father that sinners turn to Him in repentance and faith in His Son, Jesus. God sent Him forth as a propitiation—a sacrifice to turn away His righteous anger against sin—as His blood was shed and His life was given in the place of rebellious people like you and me.

We are all individuals who have broken His holy law and we stand condemned and ready to be sent to hell. But "God is now declaring to men that all people everywhere should repent, because He has fixed a day in which He will judge the world in righteousness through a Man whom He has appointed, having furnished proof to all men by raising Him from the dead" (Acts 17:30). Indeed, this Man is Jesus who said, "I am the way and the truth, and the life; no one comes to the Father but through Me" (John 14:6).

This is the gospel America despises, but it is the message people need to hear today—not *how to be delivered from the social injustice of man,* but *how to be delivered from the righteous justice of God!* We must love those who hate us and give them the good news, for "there is salvation in no one else; for there is no other name under heaven that has been given among men by which we must be saved" (Acts 4:12). We must graciously tell them, "If you

213

confess with your mouth Jesus as Lord, and believe in your heart that God raised Him from the dead, you will be saved; for with the heart a person believes, resulting in righteousness, and with the mouth he confesses, resulting in salvation. For the Scripture says, "Whoever believes in Him will not be disappointed" (Rom. 10:9–11).

It is fitting to close this chapter concerning *The Believer's Aspiration: Yearning For Heaven,* as well as to conclude this entire book with the testimony of a faithful Puritan pastor who suffered well for Christ without compromise and who longed for heaven's reward. His name was John Bunyan (1628–1688), best remembered as the author of the Christian allegory, *The Pilgrim's Progress.* His testimony reads as follows:

> Christ's death for us was so virtuous that, in the space of three days and nights, he reconciled to God in his flesh every one of God's elect. He presented himself to the justice of the law, standing in the stead, place and room of all that he undertook for, and gave his life a ransom for many, abolishing death, destroying him that had the power of death, taking away the sting of death, obtaining for us the gift of the holy Spirit, and taking possession of heaven for us! This heaven! Who knows what it is? This Glory! Who knows what it is? It is called God's throne, God's house, God's habitation, paradise, the kingdom of God, the high and holy place, Abraham's bosom, and the place of heavenly pleasures. In this heaven is to be found *the face of God forever,* immortality, the person of Christ, the prophets, angels, the revelation of all mysteries, the knowledge of all the elect, and ETERNITY. This heaven we possess already. We are in it, we are set down in it, and we partake already of the benefits through our head, the Lord Jesus. It is fit that we should believe this, rejoice in this, talk of this, tell one another of this, and live in the expectation of our own personal enjoyment of it. And as we should do all this, so we should bless and praise the name of God who has put over this house, this kingdom, and inheritance into the hand of so faithful a friend, yea, a brother and blessed Saviour. All these things are the fruit of his sufferings, and his

sufferings the fruit of his love which passes all knowledge. O how we should bow the knee before him and call him tender Father; yea, how we should love and obey him and devote ourselves unto this service, and be willing to be also sufferers for his sake, to whom be honour and glory for ever![83]

May this be the heartfelt testimony of every saint committed to *Pursuing Christlikeness in a Time of Mounting Hostility and Apathy.*

---

83   John Bunyan, *The Works of John Bunyan: The Saint's Knowledge of Christ's Love, in Works* (Glasgow, Edinburgh, London: Blackie and Son, 1855), 20.

Appendix

Indeed, as stated in chapter one, there is much more agreement than disagreement among Christians concerning God's kingdom program. But there is an ongoing debate concerning certain aspects of it, especially as it relates to the thousand-year reign of Christ in Revelation 20 (the position I hold). This is due to differing interpretive assumptions that influence how we understand language and the Bible—a science and art of interpretation called *hermeneutics*.

Some believe (as I do) that the prophetic Scriptures should be interpreted *in a literal, natural, and normal sense* (while taking into consideration figures of speech and symbols), while others believe they should be interpreted *spiritually*, being careful to look for hidden meanings embedded in some Old Testament passages and allowing later New Testament revelation to shape and inform them.

From my perspective, when interpreted in a *literal* and clear-cut manner consistent with the original message and intent of the Old Testament authors, the New Testament *continues* the narrative of the Old Testament prophets. Among other things, this means Jesus will actually reign on earth in an intermediate kingdom between His Second Coming and the final consummation of all things in the eternal state, a position known as *premillennialism*.

On the other hand, those who use a *spiritual* principle of interpretation believe the New Testament *transforms* or *transcends* the Old Testament storyline rather than *continues* it. This requires a *spiritual* interpretation whereby Jesus and the New Testament authors *reinterpret, redefine*, and *spiritualize* the kingdom message of the Old Testament. This view would therefore understand Revelation 20 as a description of the current reign of Christ in the present age, a position known as *amillennialism*. They therefore deny an intermediate kingdom and believe instead that the present church age will be followed immediately by the new heavens and new earth based on an eschatological framework known as the "two-age" model.[84]

---

84 Matt Waymeyer, *Amillennialism and the Age to Come: A Premillennial Critique of the Two-Age Model* (Woodlands, Texas: Kress Biblical Resources, 2016), 1.

Premillennialism and the Mediatorial Kingdom

As stated in chapter one, from a premillennial perspective, Scripture also affirms another aspect of God's universal kingdom, a *Mediatorial Kingdom* that can be defined as *God's sovereign rule over the earth through divinely chosen human representatives who speak on His behalf and who represent the people before Him*.[85] Here God exercises absolute authority in His invisible, spiritual kingdom on earth through the agency of divinely chosen men. He gave them special revelation that they recorded in Scripture to explain His kingdom purposes and how sinners can enter it. We see this in men like Adam, Melchizedek, Noah, Abraham, Isaac, Jacob, Joseph, Samuel, and Israel's prophets, priests, and kings like David and Solomon. He also mediated His rule through His chosen people Israel, the Old Testament witness nation, "to whom belongs the adoption as sons, and the glory and the covenants and the giving of the Law and the temple service and the promises, whose are the fathers, and from whom is the Christ according to the flesh, who is over all, God blessed forever. Amen" (Rom. 9:4–5).

However, because Israel rejected her promised Messiah and the kingdom He offered (Acts 2:22–23), Jesus judged them and said, "Therefore I say to you, the kingdom of God will be taken away from you and given to a people, producing the fruit of it" (Matt. 21:43); a reference to the *church* consisting of both Jews and Gentiles, "a chosen race, a royal priesthood, a holy nation, a people for God's own possession" (1 Peter 2:9; *cf.* Rom. 9:25–26). The church will continue to be the custodians of divine truth and mediate God's kingdom purposes until a future day when, by God's grace and in fulfillment of His unconditional promises, Israel repents, embraces her King in saving faith, and bears fruit for His kingdom (Zech. 12:10; 14:8–9; Rom. 11:2, 25–26).

We first see God's sovereign rule over the earth in the first created man, Adam, who was tasked with ruling over God's very good creation:

---

85 Alva J. McClain, *The Greatness of the Kingdom* (Winona Lake, Indiana: BMH, 1959), 41.

> Then God said, "Let Us make man in Our image, according to Our likeness; and let them *rule* over the fish of the sea and over the birds of the sky and over the cattle and over all the earth, and over every creeping thing that creeps on the earth. God created man in His own image, in the image of God He created him; male and female He created them. God blessed them; and God said to them, "Be fruitful and multiply, and fill the earth, and *subdue* it; and *rule over* the fish of the sea and over the birds of the sky and over every living thing that moves on the earth."
> (Gen 1:26–28; emphasis mine)

As a result of Adam's sin and God's curse upon him and his posterity (Rom. 5:12), he was unable to successfully discharge what God had commissioned him to do (Gen. 1:26–28)—a failure that is abundantly evident in our fallen world of confusion, corruption, and pollution. But God's Kingdom plan was not thwarted. Because He is a *sovereign* and not a *contingent* God who rules in absolute authority over all things (Isa. 46:10) and "works all things after the counsel of His will" (Eph. 1:11), *He actually ordained to allow the fall as an integral part of His plan and purpose to glorify Himself.*

We see this most vividly in what God did after Adam's fall. He set into motion a magnificent plan of redemption decreed in eternity past (Eph. 1:4) whereby he promised that a coming seed of a woman (Gen. 3:16) would not only defeat sin, Satan, and death, but also save His image bearers and restore creation into conformity with his Kingdom purposes. This was accomplished in the sacrificial death and resurrection of Jesus Christ where "He made Him who knew no sin to be sin on our behalf, so that we might become the righteousness of God in Him" (2 Cor. 5:21). There "He rescued us from the domain of darkness, and transferred us to the kingdom of His beloved Son, in whom we have redemption, the forgiveness of sins" (Col. 1:13–14).

God's Mediatorial Kingdom in the
Old and New Testaments

We see evidence of God's Kingdom plan of redemption and restoration unfolding beginning in Old Testament history where God governed the earth through a variety of mediators who served in three capacities: *prophet, priest,* and *king*—functions only the Lord Jesus Christ could ultimately fulfill. Referring to the coming Messiah, the Lord Jesus Christ, God promised to raise up a new *prophet* like Moses who would receive and preach divine revelation and lead his people (Deut. 18:15–22; *cf.* John 1:21, 25, 43–45; 6:14; 7:40); One who would also serve as *High Priest* (Ps. 110:4; Heb. 5:5–6, 10; 6:20) and *king* (Ps. 2; 110:1–4).

The New Testament then *continues* the narrative of the Old Testament prophets, helping us to understand that the *Mediatorial Kingdom* will include a literal, thousand-year reign of Christ upon the earth (Rev. 20:4–6) where he will rule as the Last Adam. This will be in fulfillment of Old Testament prophecies, which also includes a cosmic renewal of this present earth (Acts 3:21; Matt. 19:28; Rom. 8:20; Rev. 21–22) and the literal fulfillment of national and physical blessings for ethnic Israel and other Gentile nations (Gen. 12:3; 22:18; Isa. 19:16–25; Rev. 21:24, 26). Christ's millennial reign upon the earth will finally transform everything on this planet into conformity with the perfect will of God and His *Universal Kingdom*. This intermediate kingdom (between His second coming and the final consummation of all things in the eternal state) will then transition to the kingdom of the Father when "the Son Himself also will be subjected to the One who subjected all things to Him, so that God may be all in all" (1 Cor. 15:28).

The final mediatorial reign of Christ upon the earth—often called the *Millennial Reign of Christ* or the *Messianic Kingdom*—will therefore be the consummating bridge between human history and the eternal kingdom described in Revelation 21:1–22:5. As Michael Vlach asserts,

> The Bible's story line demands a future earthly reign of the Last Adam and Messiah (Jesus) upon the earth. Jesus and those who belong to Him must successfully reign *from* and

over the realm (earth) where the first Adam was tasked to rule but failed (see Gen. 1:26–28). This kingdom of the Messiah must occur before the eternal state begins when Jesus hands His successful mediatorial kingdom reign to God the Father (see 1 Cor. 15:24, 28).[86]

Covenant Fulfillments

God's *Mediatorial Kingdom* on earth is in direct fulfillment of the plans and details of four eternal and unconditional biblical covenants—the Noahic, Abrahamic, Davidic, and New covenants. Each one points to a future and final rule of King Jesus, the "Son of Man" who will succeed where Adam failed. This will allow those who are united to Him through saving faith to reign with Him (2 Tim. 2:12; Rev. 1:6; 5:10; 20:4, 6)—a reign *from* and *over* the earth as God originally intended (Matt. 19:28; Rev. 5:10). Richard Mayhew offers a succinct summary that may prove helpful in grasping the general flow of the covenant promises and how they relate to God's kingdom purposes:

> The Noahic covenant promised stability of nature so God's kingdom purposes could play out in history (Gen. 8:21–22). The Abrahamic covenant guaranteed a seed line involving Abraham and the developing people of Israel, which would be the vehicle and means for blessing the people groups of the world (Gen. 12:2–3). This covenant also promised a land for Israel (Gen. 12:6–7) that would serve as the basis for God's earthly kingdom rule and as a microcosm of what God would do for all nations (Isa. 2:2–4; 27:6). The Davidic covenant directly discussed the role of David and his descendants in establishing God's kingdom on earth, which would bless both Israel and the Gentiles (2 Sam. 7:12–19). The New covenant revealed God's plans to enable his people to love and serve him through a new heart and the indwelling Holy Spirit (Jer. 31:31–34; Ezek. 36:26–27).[87]

---

86 Michael J. Vlach, *He Will Reign Forever: A Biblical Theology of the Kingdom of God* (Silverton, Oregon: Lampion Press, 2017), 18.

87 Richard Mayhue, *Biblical Doctrine: A Systematic Summary of Bible Truth*, eds. John MacArthur and Richard Mayhue (Wheaton, Illinois: Crossway, 2017), 852.

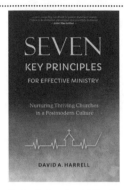

Seven Key Principles for Effective Ministry
Nurturing Thriving Churches in a Postmodern Culture
David A. Harrell

Trade Paperback, 192pp
ISBN: 9781633421301
Published by Shepherd Press

A book that exhorts and encourages Christian ministers and leaders to be committed to the principled model for successful ministry that God has established through the teaching of the New Testament.

"Dave Harrell outlines with unusual clarity the essential features of authentic church ministry. . . . Prepare to be instructed, encouraged, and powerfully motivated."—*John MacArthur*

"It is refreshing to have such a clear, direct, and powerful book."
—*Shannon Hurley*

". . . succinctly summarizes the essential principles of authentic biblical ministry."—*Phil Johnson*

"Here is a book worth reading and passing on to those just starting the journey of church leadership and ministry."
—*Conrad Mbewe*

Compact Expository Pulpit Commentary Series

A Series of Eight Mini Books
4.25 x 7 inch small format
David A. Harrell

Approximately 96pp each
Published by Great Writing Publications
www.greatwriting.org

- Finding Grace in Sorrow: Enduring Trials with the Joy of the Holy Spirit, ISBN 9781734345285
- Finding Strength in Weakness: Drawing Upon the Existing Grace Within, ISBN 9781734345247
- Glorifying God in Your Body: Seeing Ourselves from God's Perspective, ISBN 9781735949116
- God, Evil, and Suffering: Understanding God's Role in Tragedies and Atrocities, ISBN 9780960020362
- God's Gracious Gift of Assurance: Rediscovering the Benefits of Justification by Faith, ISBN 9781734345216
- Our Sin and the Savior: Understanding the Need for Renewing and Sanctifying Grace, ISBN 9781734345209
- The Marvel of Being in Christ: Adoring God's Loving Provision of New Life in the Spirit, ISBN 9781734345230
- The Miracle of Spiritual Sight: Affirming the Transforming Doctrine of Regeneration, ISBN 9781734345292

Out of the Depths

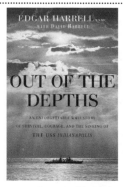

Out of the Depths: An Unforgettable WWII Story of Survival,
Courage, and the Sinking of the USS Indianapolis
David A. Harrell and Edgar Harrell

Trade Paperback, 208pp
ISBN: 9780764217647
Published by Bethany House Publishers
available from https://www.indysurvivor.com/

On July 30, 1945: After transporting uranium for the atomic bomb that would soon be dropped on Hiroshima, the USS Indianapolis headed unaccompanied toward a small island in the South Pacific. At 12:14 a.m., she was struck by two Japanese torpedoes, rolled over, and sank.

Marine survivor Edgar Harrell vividly describes the horrors of being plagued by dehydration, exposure, saline poisoning, and sharks. This is a story of courage, ingenuity, and faith in God's providence in the midst of the greatest catastrophe at sea in the history of the U.S. Navy.

"A gripping tale of men tested beyond anything they thought possible—and how they responded with bravery, endurance, and faith."
—Oliver L. North, Lt. Col., USMC (Ret.)